Birmingham Repertory Theatre Company
in association with Soho Theatre Company
presents

Perpetua
By Fraser Grace

First performance at The Door,
Birmingham Repertory Theatre
Thurs 15 April 1999

SUPPORTED BY
THE NATIONAL LOTTERY
THROUGH
THE **ARTS COUNCIL**
OF ENGLAND

Birmingham City Council WEST MIDLANDS ARTS

Providing Theatre for Birmingham

Paddy Irishman, Paddy Englishman and Paddy...?

By Declan Croghan

Thu 4 Feb - Sat 20 Feb

'What we have to do now is to focus our minds on how we are going to get ourselves out of this situation'.

Kevin and Anto are mates. They're getting by; earning a few spondoolicks, cooking enormous fry ups, avoiding the bad pint and trying desperately to understand women.

But last night a good turn turned bad, and now they've stumbled into something much bigger than both of them. The situation is exploding out of all control and their Irish past is about to come crashing in on their London lives.

Declan Croghan's hilarious black comedy looks at freedom and prejudice, heroism and cowardice and asks to whom we owe our true allegiances.

Director: Anthony Clark
Designer: Patrick Connellan
Lighting: Tim Mitchell

After Dark: Wed 17 Feb (after the perf)

Trips

By Sarah Woods

Fri 26 Feb - Sat 20 Mar

'Have you ever wondered why you find a four and a half foot tall yellow cat more comforting than your own friends?'

What happens when you lose your focus in this dazzling new land of opportunity? Nik, John, Hayley, Dan and Glen are off on a night out; drugs, clubs and the fantastic twenty four hour garage. But tonight things are not quite going to plan.

Searching for love, excitement and one infallible business idea they are all about to encounter more than they ever thought possible. And what has Princess Anne got to do with it all?.

Sarah Woods' bold, funny and technologically astonishing new play combines live performance with video to explore where we are now, and where we are all heading.

Director: Jeremy Raison
Designer: Kit Surrey

After Dark: 17 Mar (after the perf)

Nightbus

By Peter Cann

Wed 24 Mar - Sat 3 Apr

'I'm not the kind of person things happen to.'

Meet Donna. She's a tour guide on one of those open-topped Birmingham Tour buses and she knows her city. The city of 1001 trades, of the Rotunda and Spaghetti Junction: the city with more parks than Paris, more miles of canal than Venice and less fun than Dudley, or so it seems.

But Donna doesn't care. Hers is a safe life, governed by electronic organisers, regular hours and familiar routes and routines.

But tonight, fate takes a hand in launching Donna on a bus-ride into weird and unfamiliar territory: one of backstreet cosmetic surgeons and genetic engineers, of phoney traffic wardens, hotel receptionists, escaped chimpanzees, terrifying swimming instructors and crazy bargemen - all out to steal Donna's heart.

Using original, live music, five inventive performers will be brought together in this action packed comic journey for all the family - beyond the outer margins of the city we know - or think we know.

NIGHTBUS is the first of this year's Rep Community Tours funded by the Sir Barry Jackson Trust

Director: Phil Tinline
Designer: Jens Cole

After Dark: Wed 31 Mar (after the performance)

Produced in association with Soho Theatre Company

Perpetua

By Fraser Grace

Thu 15 Apr - Sat 8 May

'When a person feels betrayed by the law they trust in, they start to feel there is no way to do good 'cept by forcing themselves to do bad'

Are some lives worth more than others? The town of Pensacola, Florida is about to be set alight by the fiercest of battles. A struggle that pits the law of God against the law of the land, and the right to life against the right to choose.

On one side of the city stands May Lake abortion clinic, on the other the headquarters of the pro-life extremists Operation Freedom.

The battle rages and the stakes get higher with potentially murderous consequences. Fraser Grace's gripping new play challenges our deepest moral beliefs.

Director: Jonathan Lloyd
Designer: Timothy Meaker

After Dark: Wed 28 April (after the perf)

All That Trouble That We Had

By Paul Lucas

Thu 13 May - Sat 5 Jun

'We're only good people gone slightly desperate'

When you're in despair no action seems too extreme. On one side of a bridge a daughter employs reckless measures to secure the return of her dead mother. On the other side a man reads *Heroes of Crime* and contemplates the craziest of schemes. And always in the background the distant sound of bodies splashing down from the bridge into the river.

But what part does the cheery, cigar smoking postmistress play? And who is the overweight salesman suddenly dropped into their

lives? And are these bizarre happenings really chance, malice or destiny?
All That Trouble That We Had is a darkly comic and vivacious tale of wickedness on the margins of society celebrates the hopeless, the lonely and the unsuccessful, and explores our capricious ability to survive in vicious times.

Director: Anthony Clark

After Dark: 6 Jun (after the perf)

In the Main House

10 Days In June

4 Jun - 13 Jun

A festival of the very best in live theatre for young people - taking place all over the theatre. Highlights of the festival include a brand new musical with live animation by David Greig - *Danny 306 & Me (4 Ever)*, a fantastic updated version of *The Magic Flute*, a visit from Sooty and his friends plus much more.

Puppets, music, participation, a full programme of workshops and after show events make for a great day out at theatre.

For a full schedule of events or to receive your copy of the *10 Days In June* Festival Brochure call Box Office on 0121 236 4455.

Tickets from just £3.50

Perpetua
By Fraser Grace

CAST

Tyrone Huggins Father D

Annabelle Dowler Angela

Justin Salinger John Lemic

Nicola Redmond Rosemary

David Hounslow Richard

Jonathon Lloyd
Director

Timothy Meaker
Designer

Symon Harner
Lighting Designer

Jill McCullough
Dialect Coach

Niki Ewen Stage
Manager

Ruth Morgan
Deputy Stage Manager

Daniel Precious
Assistant Stage Manager

Fraser Grace
Author

Fraser Grace began writing for the stage whilst working for *Back to Back Theatre*, a Birmingham-based touring company for which he also acted and directed. He has subsequently worked as a freelance writer - publishing two volumes of fiction for teenagers, touring as a performance poet, and graduating from the University of Birmingham's MA Playwriting course. Both *Somebody Else* (1995) and *Dermot's Windows* (1996) were chosen for presentation in Stagecoach! New Playwriting Festivals, and a third play *Cockayne* is currently under commission here at the Rep. Fraser has served on the national executive committee of the Theatre Writer's Union, and more recently on the Writers' Guild of Great Britain theatre committee. *Perpetua* was joint winner of the 1996 Verity Bargate Award. The author would like to thank Theresa Heskins, Paul Sirett and John Burgess for their help in developing this play.

Author's Note

Is there anyone or anything you would willingly kill or die for?

In the United States a battle has been joined. On one side, people who believe abortion is murder are determined to stop the 'baby-killers'. On the other, those who see 'terminations' as 'a regrettable necessity' fight equally hard to preserve the 'right to choose'. The upshot is a protracted and violent struggle in which clinics have been firebombed, doctors shot dead, 'protesters' put on death row, and the law itself twisted inside and out in an effort to end the killing.

Could the same thing happen in the UK? Are our democratic rights, rights for everyone, or just those who agree with the majority? How do you stand up for something you believe in when the law is used to suppress peaceful protest? Isn't right to freedom of expression just a charter for terrorists?

It will be clear from these questions, and from the quotation marks above, that this war is not only a war of actions but of rhetoric. Of violent words and disturbing, sometimes appalling images.

I wanted to know how the conflict got to such a pitch, and in particular, how people so committed to the sanctity of life could find themselves picking up a gun with the sole intent of killing. *Perpetua* is the result.

Recent cases of abortion-related violence:

March 10 1993: Penascola, Florida:
Dr. David Gunn is shot to death outside a clinic, becoming the first U.S doctor killed during an anti-abortion demonstration. Michael Griffin is convicted and is serving a life sentence.

August 1993: Wichita, Kansas:
Dr. George Tiller is shot in the arm as he drives out of the parking lot at his clinic, Rachelle 'Shelley' Shannon is convicted and sentenced to 11 years in prison.

July 29 1994: Penascola, Florida.
Dr. John Bayard Britton and his volunteer escort, James H. Barrett, are slain outside an abortion clinic. Barrett's wife, June, is wounded in the attack. Paul J. Hill, 40, a former minister and anti-abortion activist, is convicted of murder and sentenced to death.

November 8 1994: Vancouver, British Columbia:
Dr. Garson Romalis, who performs abortions is shot in the leg while eating breakfast at home.

December 30 1994: Boston:
John Salvi opens fire with a rifle inside two Boston-area abortion clinics, killing two receptionists and wounding five others. Sentenced to life without parole, he kills himself in prison in 1996.

January 16 1997: Atlanta:
Two bomb blasts an hour apart rock an Atlanta building containing an abortion clinic. Seven people are injured. Eric Rudolph is charged by federal authorities in October 1998.

January 29 1998: Birmingham, Alabama:
A bomb explodes outside a Birmingham abortion clinic. An off-duty police officer is killed and a nurse critically injured in the first fatal bombing of a U.S abortion clinic. Eric Rudolph is charged but eludes a massive manhunt.

October 23, 1998: Amherst, New York:
A sniper kills Dr, Barnett Slepian, by firing a shot through the physician's window, the first fatality among five sniper attacks on New York or Canadian abortion providers over four years.

March 14, 1999:
Bomb explodes outside a women's clinic in Asheville, North Carolina. No injuries are caused because the device only partially detonates.

soho theatre company

Soho Theatre company has a twenty five year history of producing new plays and discovering new writers. The company premiered the early work of such writers as Caryl Churchill, David Edgar, Pam Gems, Tanika Gupta, Barrie Keeffe, Hanif Kureishi, Tony Marchant, Diane Samuels, Sue Townsend and Timberlake Wertenbaker.

Through its extensive research and development programme the company encourages writers at every stage of their career. By reporting on scripts, running workshops, one to one sessions, rehearsed readings, awards and commissions we work to develop writers and their scripts before taking them into production with Soho Theatre Company or other theatres.

We are delighted that *Perpetua* by Fraser Grace is being produced at the Birmingham Rep in association with Soho Theatre. The play won our biennial competition for new writers, The Verity Bargate Award, in 1996 and has been in development with the company.

In 1996 the company bought a building in Dean Street with National Lottery money, through the Arts Council of England, which is currently under construction. The new Soho Theatre and Writers' Centre at 21 Dean Street, is due to open its doors within the next 12 months. This £10.6 million project will include a flexible theatre, bar, restaurant, offices, rehearsal rooms and uniquely, space for writers and individual writers' rooms, facilities from scripts surgeries, workshops and rehearsed reading. Everything we need to house our bold artistic policy under one roof.

'Soho Theatre Company has found a new home, and it promises to be one of London's coolest places for hot new talent' Time Out

If you have enjoyed *Perpetua* and would like to find out more about the company's work with writers, or join our mailing list contact us at:
21 Dean St, London, W1V 6NE

HYPERLINK mail to:
sara@sohotheatre.com.

If you can help us raise the final £85,000 please contact Zoe Reed on 0171 5060 or at HYPERLINK mail to:
zoe@sohotheatre.com .

Tyrone Huggins
Father Dave

For Birmingham Repertory Theatre: Eddie in *Season's Greetings*; Crooks in *Of Mice & Men*

Theatre: Trevor Avery in *Absence of War* (Royal National Theatre); Jason in *Murmuring Judges* (Royal National Theatre); Gabriel in *Fences* (Garrick Theatre); Cornelius and Washington Junior in *Iced* (Black Theatre Co-Op and Nottingham Playhouse); Julius in *Time and the Room* (Nottingham Playhouse); Francis Barber in *Resurrection* (Bush Theatre); Sanda in *Beatification of Area Boy* (West Yorkshire Playhouse); Performer in *The Desire Paths* (Graeme Miller Company Tour/Royal Court); Scruple/Pearmain in *The Recruiting Officer* (Manchester Library); Black Caesar/Tench in *Our Country's Good* (Manchester Library); Don Madariaga in *The Four Horsemen of the Apocalypse* (Glasgow Citizens); Various in *The Gods are not to Blame* (Talawa Theatre). Co-founder of Impact Theatre co-operative.

TV: *Dangerfield*; *Hetty Wainthropp*; *Backup*; *Casualty*; *Book Box Thief*; *All or Nothing*; *Giving Tongue*; *Absence of War*; *The Bill*; *Sharp End*; *Bergerac*; *Travelling Man*; *Emmerdale Farm*; *Urban Jungle*.

Angela
Annabelle Dowler

Born: Merseyside
Trained: University of Bristol & Webber Douglas (Academy of Dramatic Art)
First appearance for Birmingham Repertory Theatre.

Annabelle spent a year touring Spain with the English Theatre Workshop before going to drama school. Since graduating last year she has worked with the Soho Theatre Company and has recently portrayed Liza in *Peter Pan* at the Royal National Theatre.

Justin Salinger
John Lemic

Born: London
Trained: Guildhall School of Music & Drama
First Appearance for Birmingham Repertory Theatre.

Theatre: Peter Pan in *Peter Pan* (National Theatre), Borachio in *Much Ado About Nothing* (Cheek by Jowl), Dickie in *Chips With Everything* (National Theatre), Candide in *Candide* (The Gate), Nephew/Youth in *Dona Rosita The Spinster* (Almeida Theatre), *Salome* and *Early Morning* (National Studio), Frankie in *Dealer's Choice* (National Theatre).

Film: Velvet Goldmine

Nicola Redmond
Rosemary

Born: Glasgow
Trained: Central School of Speech & Drama
First appearance for Birmingham Repertory Theatre.

Theatre: *Shang-A-Lang* (Bush Theatre); Jane Austen and Mr Knightley in *Emma* (Gilded Balloon); *With Love From Nicolae* (Bristol Old Vic/Teatrul Dramatic, Romania); *Waking*, *Children of the Dust*, *Me & My Friend* (Soho Theatre); *The Baby*, *Phoenix* (Bush Theatre); *Bearing Fruit* (Hampstead Theatre); *Rag Doll*, *Where's Willy?* (Bristol Old Vic); *Death & The Kings Horseman* (Manchester Royal Exchange); *The Good Sisters* (Sheffield Crucible); *The Orphan's Comedy* (Traverse Theatre); Elizabeth I in *Vivat Vivat Regina*, (Pitlochry); Gypsy in *Beaux Stratagem*, Lady Macduff in *Macbeth* and Imogen Parrott in *Trelawney of the Wells* (Royal National Theatre).

West End: Julia in *Cheek by Jowl's The Duchess of Malfi* (Wyndhams/World Tour); Christine in *Body and Soul* (Albery).

TV/Film: *Casualty*; *Gooseberries Don't Dance*; *Eastenders*; *The Phoenix & the Carpet*; *Silent Witness* (Series II); *Ruth Rendell's Secret House of Death*; *Goodnight Sweetheart*; *The Case of Esther Pay*; *Pie In The Sky*; *Capital Sins*; *Three, Seven, Eleven* (series 1 and 2); *Family*; *Harry's Kingdom*; *Boy Soldier*; *Morphine & Dolly Mixtures*.

David Hounslow
Richard

Trained: Manchester Polytechnic School of Theatre
First Appearance for Birmingham Repertory Theatre.

Theatre: *The Snowman* (Leicester Haymarket); *Othello* (RSC); *Henry V* (RSC); *Coriolanus* (RSC); *The Wives' Excuse* (RSC); *Zenobia* (RSC); *Bent* (Royal National Theatre); *Treasure Island* (Farnham Redgrave); *Billy Budd* (Sheffield Crucible); *Fuente Ovejuna* (Royal National Theatre); *Our Boys* (Cockpit Theatre); Danum in *All of You Mine* (The Bush).

TV: *The Unknown Soldier*; *True Blues*; *Coronation Street*; *Othello*; *Children of the North*; *Gone to the Dogs*; *The Bill*; *Resnick*; *True Crimes*; *Minder*; *Bad Company*; *Under the Hammer*; *Anna Lee*; *Soldier Soldier*; *Deadly Crack*; *The Cinder Path*; *The Prisoner*; *Chandler and Co.*; *Six Sides of Coogan*; *Crimes and Punishment*; *Turning World*; *Is It Legal*; *Peak Practice*; *A Wing and a Prayer*; *Dangerfield*; *Playing the Field*; *The Unknown Soldier*; *Bugs*; *Crimewatch*; *Within Living Memory*; *Casualty*; *Eastenders* and *City Central*.

Film: *London Kills Me*; *Feverpitch*; *The Man Who Knew Too Little*; *I Want You*.

Radio: *Cabs* (Piccadilly Radio, Manchester)

Jonathon Lloyd
Director

Currently Associate Director at Soho Theatre Company, where he has directed *The Backroom*, *Belle Fontaine* and *Skeleton*, and run an Under-11s playwriting scheme.

Other productions include *Summer Begins* (RNT Studio/Donmar), Channel Four Sitcom Festival (Riverside Studios), *Serving It Up* (Bush), *Blood Knot* (Gate) and *Function of the Orgasm* (Finborough).

As a writer for children's television: *Dog and Duck* (ITV).

Timothy Meaker
Designer

Trained in architecture at the University of Liverpool and in Theatre Design at the Court Theatre.

Recently Tim has worked as resident designer at the Maddermarket Theatre, Norwich where his designs included *The Glass Menagerie*, *The Broken Jug* and *Too Many Ghosts*.

Other recent productions include *Miss Julie* at the Turtle Key Arts Centre, *Twelfth Night* at the Chelsea Centre; *Pippin* at the Bridewell, *Immaterial Times* at the White Bear and *This Wretched Splendour* at the Grace Theatre.

In 1997 Tim designed a very successful production of *Woyzeck* directed by Sarah Kane at the Gate Theatre. Also at the Gate *In the Solitude of the Cotton Fields* and *Bug with Hire Gun TC*. He designed *Eat an Apple a Day* (National School Tour) and *Romeo and Juliet* at the Prince Theatre.

Symon Harner
Lighting Designer

Lighting Designs include: for the Birmingham Repertory Theatre;
The world premieres of *The Tenant of Wildfell Hall* and *East Lynne*, *A Shaft of Sunlight* (For Tamasha Theatre Company), *Playing By The Rules* (also at the Drill Hall, London), *Turn of the Screw*, National Tours of *Metamorphosis* and *Kafka's Dick* (the latter being in collaboration with Lennie Tucker),*The Trial* (for The Mouse People) and *The Canal Ghost*.

For the Birmingham Rep Youth Workshop; *Pinocchio*, *The Threepenny Opera*, Tony Harrison's *'V'*, and *The Magic Toyshop* (also at the Edinburgh Festival in collaboration with Philip Swoffer.)

For Plymouth Theatre Royal; *Tales From the Vienna Woods* and *The Hired Man*.

Most recently Symon designed the lighting for *Trips*, and the 'Transmissions' festival in The Door.

Production Credits:

With thanks to:
C.K. Cosmetics Uk Ltd., Sunrise Medical, Moet & Chandon, Sainsbury's plc, B.P.A.S., Thorntons, Herbal smoking mix donated by Honeyrose products Ltd., Pedigree Pet Foods, David Manners parts for Jaguar & Daimler cars, Chupa Chups.

New Work at Birmingham Repertory Theatre
- past, present and future

In recent years, Birmingham Repertory Theatre has produced a range of popular, award-winning and critically acclaimed new plays. These include *Divine Right* (1996), Peter Whelan's timely examination of the future of the British monarchy, Debbie Isitt's *Squealing Like a Pig* (1996), Nick Stafford's *The Whisper of Angels' Wings* (1997) and Ayub Khan-Din's *East is East* (1996), a co-production with Tamasha Theatre Company and the Royal Court Theatre, London.

In 1998, Bill Alexander's production of *Frozen* by Bryony Lavery, which starred Anita Dobson, Tom Georgeson and Josie Lawrence, was unanimously praised for its bravery, humanity and humour in exploring the intertwined experiences of a mother, the murderer of her daughter and the psychiatrist who treats him. *Frozen* went on to win the 1998 TMA Barclays Theatre Award for Best New Play.

In the Autumn, thanks to funding from the Arts Council's Stabilisation Scheme, we were able to start programming our former studio space – now renamed The Door – with a year round programme of new work. Opening with the appropriately named *Confidence* by Judy Upton and followed by Maureen Lawrence's *Twins* and Kate Dean's *Down Red Lane*, the theatre aims to provide a challenging, entertaining and diverse season of ten new plays, including two that tour to arts centres and community venues in the West Midlands.

In support of this work the theatre also runs an extensive education and development programme. Two of the plays in this season: Declan Croghan's

Confidence: Jody Watson as Ella, Robin Pirongs as Ben, Zoot Lynam as Dean.
Photo: Tristram Kenton

Paddy Irishman, Paddy Englishman and Paddy...? and *Trips* by Sarah Woods started life on the theatre's attachment scheme for writers. Beginning with just an outline or initial idea for a play, the writer works together with other professional practitioners including actors, directors and designers at appropriate stages throughout the writing process, with the ultimate goal a production of the play at this theatre.

Also in the Autumn, the Education and Literary Departments worked together to present *Transmissions*, a project in which young people from across the city of Birmingham, and from the ages of 7 - 25 wrote and presented their own plays with the support of professional playwrights, directors and actors.

If you would like more information on this or other aspects of our work, please contact us on
Tel: 0121 236 6771 x 2108/2104
Ben Payne
Literary Manager

The Birmingham Repertory Theatre gratefully acknowledges the support of the Sir Barry Jackson Trust in its new work development programme

Supported by
THE
SIR BARRY JACKSON
TRUST

From Stage to Page

An opportunity for students to participate in the process of putting on a season of new plays. Access to the country's most contemporary theatre writers, and a chance to work with directors, actors and qualified teachers in exploring a season of cutting edge theatre - PERPETUA by Fraser Grace, ALL THAT TROUBLE WE HAD by Paul Lucas and NIGHTBUS by Peter Cann.

What's On Offer?

Workshops

On making block bookings, two workshops will be offered. The first involves an exploration of the content of the text; themes and structure etc. to be led by the Rep's Education Department and held at your college. The second will be run by a writer and the Rep's Associate Director Anthony Clark, and will explore ideas behind the writing and the process of producing the piece from page to stage. These second workshops will take place at the theatre.

After Darks

You can choose to come to the shows which are followed by an After Dark (although you are free to choose when you want to come). This is an opportunity to get the performer's perspective first hand, and to capitalise on that immediate response ensuring that your students get the most out of their time at the theatre.

Scripts

Scripts will be published for each play in a programme format. This provides an opportunity for further study of the text's form and content. Each student has their own copy of each play, at the equivalent of just £1.00. (These texts retail at £6.99).

Discounted Tickets

Tickets are available at the equivalent of just £3 per performance. With tickets normally at £9/£7, this represents a huge discount.

Unbeatable Value

Tickets for all three shows, scripts for each student, workshops with directors, writers and teachers and aftershow discussions with the company are included in the price. Stage to Page is a pro-active approach to serve mutual needs. An opportunity to tackle your curriculum in a unique, accessible way. Suitable for students of Culture, Theatre Arts, English etc.

The complete package works out at only £15 (minimum 15 students, no maximum).

What previous participants have said:
'My students don't usually have access to a professional director. It's brilliant'
'This has been the best part of the course for these students...I'm bowled over by the response. Terrific.'
'I really got to understand how complicated it is...I was much more into it because I'd read it...It was great'

For further details or to book please contact Rachel Gartside, Head of Education on 0121 236 6771

Transmissions: young playwrights

Communication, engagement and the start of something new

As Birmingham's only venue dedicated entirely to new writing, The Door is investing in writers of the future. In Autumn 1998 we launched the first part of our project with plays written by 7-25 year olds with staged readings and performances in our new writing house The Door. Short plays were developed in primary schools and through the Rep's young people's playwriting groups, led by professional writers and directors.

Those taking part in **Transmissions** explored writing, speaking, acting and reading their work with the guidance of professionals at every stage in the process. They developed their imaginative and technical skills in creating stories from action, speech and character.

In December the workshops culminated in a festival of performances. Examples of the extracts and scenes we presented include: *Wish you were here* by Modssor Rashid about a man's past returning to haunt him following his release from prison; Adam Godwin's *The Shop* which centred on the conflict of creativity and responsibility; and *Crossroads* by Sharlene Ferguson in which the friendship between two young women is placed on the line following a night on the town and an unexpected revelation. In all we presented twenty-eight pieces of writing over a two week period.

Photos: Alan Wood

There will be further **Transmissions** projects, including the continuation of the Rep's young playwright's group, which is now entering its third year. Many young playwrights from this group have gone on to develop their writing through higher education courses such as Theatre Arts or Drama at University.

What previous participants have said:

'Shy children came out of themselves and they all contributed to the script. Children and parents thoroughly enjoyed the whole experience'
TEACHER

'I learnt a lot about the hard work that is put into writing a play'
VINETA JAIN, SWANSHURST SCHOOL

'Helpful encouraging, insightful, inspiring'
TIM JEFFRIES, YOUNG WRITER

'Thank you for the chance to work with some inspiring young people'
MAYA CHOWDHRY, WRITER

'Young writers were exposed to a lot of talented professionals, inspired and encouraged to work and to believe in themselves. A lot of young people from the local community benefited.'
(THERESA HESKINS, FREELANCE DIRECTOR).

'The festival has given me practical tools to write my plays'
ADAM GODWIN, YOUNG WRITER

For more information please contact;
Rachel Gartside / Liz Ingrams on
0121 236 6771 ext 2142/2104

The Birmingham RepertoryTheatre Company
Introducing

The Door

Since it was founded in 1913 Birmingham Repertory Theatre Company has been a leading national company. Its programming has introduced a range of new and foreign plays to the British theatre repertoire, and it has been a springboard for many internationally famous actors, designers and directors.

Now the company can present classic, new and discovery plays on a scale appropriate to one of the largest acting spaces in Europe, as well as a consistent programme of new theatre in its studio, by some of the brightest contemporary talent .To celebrate this, the space has a new name and a new look.

The Door's programme seeks to find a young and culturally diverse audience for the theatre, through the production of new work in an intimate, flexible space - work, that reflects, defines and enhances their experience of the world while introducing them to the possibilities of the medium.

Confidence: Jody Watson as Ella, Robin Pirongs as Ben
Photo: Tristram Kenton

Twins: Amelda Brown as Mimi and Anne White as Gigi
Photo: Tristram Kenton

Down Red Lane: Mathew Wait as Spider
Photo: Tristram Kenton

As the arts in Birmingham have grown in stature, with the opening of Symphony Hall, the achievements of the City of Birmingham Symphony Orchestra and the arrival of the Birmingham Royal Ballet so there has been massive investment in the resident theatre company.

'Birmingham...the workshop of the theatre world."
Michael Billington - The Guardian

PERPETUA

Fraser Grace

OBERON BOOKS
LONDON

First published in 1999 by Oberon Books Ltd.
(incorporating Absolute Classics)
521 Caledonian Road, London N7 9RH
Tel: 0171 607 3637 / Fax: 0171 607 3629

e-mail: oberon.books@btinternet.com

A catalogue record for this book is available from the British Library.

ISBN 1 84002 122 5

Cover design: Andrzej Klimowski

Typography: Richard Doust

Printed in Great Britain by MPG Ltd., Bodmin.

Characters

ROSEMARY

Doctor Rosemary Bright. British, brought up and educated in Edinburgh, Scotland. A gynaecologist working in private clinics in Pensacola, Florida.

JOHN

Non-threatening build, quietly good-looking.

RICHARD

A part-time artist living in Pensacola. Pays his rent by delivering pizza – often to Doctor Bright at the clinic.

ANGELA

'Poor white southern trash.' Thin, pretty, an enthusiastic member of Operation Freedom.

FATHER D

A former pastor from one of the Pentacostal denominations in the deep South. Black, greying, overweight.

Scenes

Part One

One: Rosemary's office at the May Lake clinic
Two: Top floor office of Operation Freedom's HQ
Three: Lecture theatre, Vancouver
Four: Rosemary's office
Five: Basement of O.F.'s HQ

Part Two

Six: Basement of O.F.'s HQ
Seven: University SCR
Eight: Basement of O.F.'s HQ
Nine: Rosemary's office

Music suggested for the play is taken from various early eighties Dylan albums: *Slow Train Coming, Saved, Shot of Love.*

Place: the play is set in Pensacola, Florida USA, and briefly in Vancouver, Canada.
Time: yesterday, today, or tomorrow.

PART ONE

Scene One

A room in the US – luxurious, but somehow sterile. A window, with a blind, near which, a couch. A desk, a filing cabinet. Upstage-left a connecting door, leading to an ensuite shower room. Downstage left another door, leading to the hall. On the floor, centre stage in front of the desk, a body lies face-up, dressed in denims and motorcycle boots. The upper body is covered with a white coat.

Door opens, stage left. Enter ROSEMARY, carrying a briefcase. She is smartly and soberly dressed. She is British. She sees the body. Pause. She closes the door behind her. She puts the briefcase on the desk, with her eyes still on the body. She goes into the shower room. We hear a tap running. The body begins to moan, and an erection is simulated, using a toilet brush inserted into the sleeve of the white coat. Returning with a glass of water, she observes this without surprise, then walks to the body, takes a sip from the glass. The coat is pulled down from RICHARD's face. He smiles, and she reciprocates.

RICHARD: Hi, doc.

She smiles back, then tips the glass of water onto his face.

RICHARD: Shit!

Whassat for?

ROSEMARY: Wrong day.

ROSEMARY goes to the window and parts the blind, and looks out.

RICHARD: Great.

So. I came early. We'll get help.

ROSEMARY turns back in.

ROSEMARY: I smell pizza. Where is it?

RICHARD: Like you said, doc. Wrong day.

He kisses her.

ROSEMARY: I can taste pizza.

RICHARD: So, either you were late, or the pizza
left early.

ROSEMARY: Or you were early which we've already
established, and you ate the lot.
You did. Bastard.

RICHARD: What – you mean the suits didn't serve
afternoon tea today?

She takes off her jacket.

RICHARD: Y'know doc, I did bring another gift.

ROSEMARY: Really. Beside the obvious?

RICHARD: Now you mention that ...

*He has picked up the toilet brush and is reprising
the 'erection'.*

ROSEMARY: I have paperwork to do.

RICHARD: Paperwork.

His 'erection' collapses.

RICHARD: Maybe you don't deserve my gift. Maybe
I'll keep it.

She opens her briefcase, takes out several papers.

ROSEMARY: Fine.
Unless it's chocolate.

RICHARD: Chocolate. Every woman's dream gift.
So how's it cookin', doc. They still all jumpin' on the
devil's head out there?

ROSEMARY: Noisy. Atavistic.

RICHARD: Ata-what?

ROSEMARY: Faces like thunder, fists like knives.

*He parts the blind and peers out as she prepares
to work.*

RICHARD: Oh, you saddos. Wrinkle your face an' fuck
all comes out.
You should go the whole thing, get this place sight-
proofed. Wouldn't have to watch those goldfish
all day.

ROSEMARY: We don't. That's why we have the blind.

RICHARD: You know it was Baby-On-A-Stick-Week?
Man you should see these things. A baby on a stick.
Blood all down their little faces.
Clients, I guess.
She eyeballs him.
RICHARD: So?
ROSEMARY: So what?
RICHARD: C'mon Rosie.
ROSEMARY: Come on where?
RICHARD: Are you going to tell me, or do I have to beg?
ROSEMARY: Beg away, pizzaman.
Beat.
ROSEMARY: The Supreme Court accepts our petition.
Surprised?
RICHARD: No shit.
ROSEMARY: They call it Rycko.
RICHARD: I think you'll find they call it Reeco.
ROSEMARY: Whatever.
RICHARD: You know, I might not be able to come up
here much longer. Guys down town knew I was
sweatin' out my afternoons with the Reecoh-woman
they might see me in a different light.
ROSEMARY: You mean there's someone round here
you haven't told about us?
RICHARD: There's my wife.
So that's it, huh. Three months hard schmoozing,
case over.
ROSEMARY: That's it. I am back to work.
RICHARD: The wheel crushes the beetle, the truck
rolls on.
ROSEMARY: Interruptions notwithstanding.
Absolutely.
Pause. RICHARD checks his watch.
RICHARD: How many a those death warrants you
gonna sign, Dr Bright? I gotta shift my hot an'
spicy.
ROSEMARY: I could add one, if you like.

23

Beat.

RICHARD: We should talk.

ROSEMARY: Gift first, talk later. Or do you want to discuss my commission fee. I did sell one painting last month.

RICHARD: They torched three more clinics upstate, you hear?

No response.

Torched. Three more. Clinics.

They.

ROSEMARY: You missed one. Upstate.

Hurts to lose in my experience.

RICHARD: Yeah? When was that. When was the last time Rosie lost anything.

Virginity, right.

He lights a cigarette, takes a drag, exhales and watches the smoke toward the ceiling. Pause. ROSIE answers without looking up.

ROSEMARY: It's okay. We're safe from the bells of hell. There's a built-in tolerance. I turn it off when you come.

RICHARD: I came early.

ROSEMARY: Like you said – We'll get help.

Pause.

RICHARD: You know, these guys don't fuck around, Rosie.

ROSEMARY: Well. It's an option.

RICHARD: That why you're workin' late? Showin' you don't care?

ROSEMARY: Five o'clock, Richard. Not even that. See?

RICHARD: No-one else is around, I coulda bin anyone.

ROSEMARY: You're no-one, I made that quite clear to security. Where's my gift?

Beat.

RICHARD: Don't get mad, okay. Cheap and cheerful.

He moves to the desk and pulls the drawer open.

A pause.

ROSEMARY: Get it out of here. Now.

RICHARD: Rosie, I was loaded, I don't have a pass,
I walked right in here...

ROSEMARY: I don't believe this.

RICHARD: I walked right in, fer godsake...

ROSEMARY: Well you can walk right out. I don't
want it.

RICHARD: What? Pull round the wagons and pass
the injunctions?
Five dollars more buys one would stop a rhino. Not
a poster this time, not superglue for the doorlocks.
Not even foetus stuff through the mailbox like
Doreen gets every fucking weekend. I entered the
building with a gun. You don't juss lose the argument
with these people. Okay?

ROSEMARY: Doreen is out, Roger's giving a paper,
I was in court. Plus it's summer, plus it's broad
daylight, plus it's a clinic, not an airbase. Stop
projecting your anxiety.

RICHARD: Maybe this is something weird. Maybe it's
concern. Yeah. Maybe you can get that if you have
unprotected sexual relations.

ROSEMARY: That – was a one off.
Get rid of it, Richard.

RICHARD: Okay. You want this outa of sight?
He shuts the drawer.

ROSEMARY: When I came in here I was feeling happy.
Pause.
When the Reecoh actions start, they'll run for cover.
It's the lawyers who need to watch out, not us.

RICHARD: Lawyer, doctor, soldier, sailor, who the fuck
cares. It only takes one stiff ta get the ball rolling.
Did they ask for a volunteer at your Planned
Parenting Action Group yet?

ROSEMARY: We're going for obstructing interstate
trade. Failing that we'll have them for conspiracy.
Apparently it's already in the penal code. Somewhere.

RICHARD: Say that again?

ROSEMARY: Crowds of protesters deter people from coming in here, ergo, the people who organise these demonstrations – and all their other delights – are committing America's number one crime: obstructing trade. If they obstruct interstate trade we can get triple damages and freeze their assets. Turns out American law is just like they say. The best money can buy.

RICHARD: Interstate trade? These kids come to you from all over, huh.

ROSEMARY: Thass right pizzaman – she pulls 'em in, she pulls 'em out. Anyway they're not kids, they're women.

RICHARD: Reecoh stops them blocking the sidewalk, right. Then when they're sittin' round the kitchen table sayin' hey what else we gonna do – you do 'em for conspiracy?

ROSEMARY: Yes. Ten years in prison should test their faith pretty thoroughly.

RICHARD: Ten fucking years? Jesus.

ROSEMARY: You feel sorry for them now, do you?

RICHARD picks one of the files off the desk, stands reading it. Pause.

RICHARD: Little Charley-Anne here forgot to tick the parental consent box. We let her off with five years or what?

ROSEMARY: Richard.

RICHARD: Ten fuckin' years fer wavin' a stick-baby?

ROSEMARY: A moment ago they were torching clinics.

We do do other work. Not that anyone would notice.

She snatches the file back.

Mrs Perlman happens to have an ovarian cyst.

Pause. RICHARD walks around to the blind again, and peers through without speaking.

RICHARD: Ovarian, caesarian... You Capricorn, right?

He begins to whistle tunelessly through his teeth.
ROSEMARY can stand it no longer.

ROSEMARY: Do me a favour.

RICHARD: That's why I'm here, doc.
What?

ROSEMARY: Take a shower.

RICHARD: Take a what?

ROSEMARY: Take a shower.

RICHARD: Take a hike, lady.

ROSEMARY: I am going to finish this. Then, as it's
been a long day, and as I do have every right to be
celebrating, I might – might – change my mind.

RICHARD: About the gun, right?

ROSEMARY: About your delivery. Although fast and
friendly is not quite what I had in mind.

RICHARD: I'm showering.
It's kinda hot in here anyway. The white heat of success.
RICHARD begins to undress, hanging his clothes
on the door.

ROSEMARY: Yes well. That's why I don't need your gift.

RICHARD: Say again?

Beat. She pulls open the drawer.

ROSEMARY: If they say we don't respect life, and
I start playing Rambo, I'd say that proved their
point, wouldn't you?

RICHARD: What's wrong with a little hypocrisy once
in a while. You know hypocrisy's okay if you're
sincere about it.
Readers Digest 1964.
I even know some of these people.

ROSEMARY: Really.

RICHARD: They just 'ornery folks y'know; mamas,
papas, mental defectives. All itchin' ta take out the
devil's handmaid.

ROSEMARY: I am not the one breaking the law.

RICHARD: 'Course. Neither were they, till you paid off
the law.

ROSEMARY: We're going to use the law so it's not fair?

RICHARD: Rosie, they're the fuck-heads. Okay? Know what I say? I say think clear and play safe. The law takes care of the criminal, the rhino-stopper takes care of you.

ROSEMARY: Bullshit. When people say be careful, it's them who are scared.

RICHARD: Rosie, scared is reasonable. Scared is fucking sane. Three clinics torched upstate. Don't freeze in the headlights, respond to the situation.

ROSEMARY: With a gun? Suddenly I do feel frightened. They should sign you.

RICHARD: Yeah, they tried a couple of times. We had to share things at our school. I got the brain. You do not have to be like them to fight them.

ROSEMARY: This is what I do, Richard. I am not going to let that be a crime. And I'm not going to tool up. I happen to be proud of what I do.

RICHARD: An interesting choice of words.

ROSEMARY: I mean it.

You think it's easy to do this, do you?

RICHARD: I guess the trick is, don't think.

ROSEMARY: I meant technically. Most surgeons can see what they're doing. Not us. I've done hundreds and I haven't lost one patient – I'm not interested, I don't give a fuck for politics. All I want to do is continue the work I'm good at.

RICHARD: You know what they'll say to that. All Dahmer wanted was a friend round for tea.

Think I look like the guy with the Levi's?

ROSEMARY: Not much.

RICHARD: Me neither.

(*Singing*) Born too small for her to love me...

You comin' in here?

ROSEMARY: Possibly. When I finish what I came back here to do. God knows I wish I hadn't.

He goes into the shower room, carrying the pile of clothes and closing the door behind him. The sound of the shower is heard.

RICHARD: (*Off*) Shit!

Hell maybe you're right. People don't realise the good work goes on here. You should launch a – what they call it – a charm offensive. Show everybody the human side of baby-cide. Yessir. Every abortionist is somebody's husband, daughter, sister or friend. We just lonely people wantin' ta meet other lonely people; show 'em a good time an' a sharp blade. Let's hear it fer the slice crew. We are the stormtroopers of the gynaecological movement. I am the motha with the sucka, the wife with the knife, and for my last record I choose the King of Rock and Roll himself and 'Cut me loose'!

Pause. He slips. A smile flashes across her face.

(*Off*) Shit.

Pause. RICHARD puts his head round the door.

You know, me an' Eric are havin' a great time in here. You don't come soon, he's gonna beat you to it.

ROSEMARY: One minute pizza boy. Anyway it's turn, not cut.

RICHARD: Y' know, I'd prefer you callin' me 'Mr Artist'. What's cut?

ROSEMARY: Turn me loose. How much have you drunk today, Mr Pizza Artist?

RICHARD: Don't worry about us doc, we can stand to attention.

ROSEMARY: One minute. Alright?

RICHARD: You hear that boy? You're time is comin'. Down boy, woah there.

RICHARD has closed the door again. ROSIE gives up trying to work. She stretches back in her chair. RICHARD speaks from offstage.

(*Off*) I've bin thinkin' anyway. Maybe I'm gonna take you away from all this.

ROSEMARY: (*To herself*) Really.

RICHARD: (*Off*) That one you sold last month? Thass just the start. I got a letter. Yours truly is officially part of the Florida New Wave. My West Coast agent – you still listenin?

ROSEMARY: I'm here.

ROSEMARY picks up her white coat, slips it on. She opens a desk-drawer, takes off her knickers and drops them in.

RICHARD: (*Off*) My West Coast man says there's money in them there oils.

ROSEMARY: Is that right.

RICHARD: (*Off*) Course, if you gonna be my woman full-time you're gonna have ta start dressin' weird, sleep around some, smoke all kindsa strange substances. We artists are real bohemian.

ROSEMARY: Sounds good.

RICHARD: (*Off*) I don't think your daddy would like that.

ROSEMARY: What?

RICHARD: (*Off*) Think your old man woulda approved of Li'l Dickie Fiske? I don't think so. The Scottish Kildare would not appreciate that.

Pause.

She waits, listening.

ROSEMARY: You okay in there? Richard?

RICHARD: (*Off*) I'm just gettin' this gift o' yours nice and ready...

Pause. She moves silently to the door and snatches it open suddenly. RICHARD, wearing a towel, is framed in the doorway, with a bottle of champagne. He fires the cork at her.

RICHARD: Yee-haah!

RICHARD: What's with the white coat, doc?

ROSEMARY: You bastard.

RICHARD: Guess it's like they say, huh. Abortionists do it on demand.

Bad joke. You okay?

ROSEMARY: Great.

Pause.

RICHARD: C'mon, let's celebrate 'her return to normal life...'

ROSEMARY: Listen. I'm going home.

RICHARD: Hey look...

ROSEMARY: It's late. I'm tired.

RICHARD: Hey Rosie, I didn't mean... Hey, come on... I got pepperoni...

ROSEMARY: Take it out, Richard, get rid of it. I mean the gun.

RICHARD: Okay. Okay.

Do I get to get dressed first?

She takes off the white coat.

ROSEMARY: In Britain we have apathy, toleration. Why can't bloody Americans think of something more civilised than killing their opponents?

RICHARD: You really wanna know the answer to that?

ROSEMARY: Actually, yes.

RICHARD: Maybe it goes back ta the way we had ta solve our biggest fight.

ROSEMARY: I'm sorry?

RICHARD: The American War of Independence.

ROSEMARY: O please.

RICHARD: (*Arch*) Hell doc – you don't like our country, y'all better kill some other fucker's babies.

Pause.

Hey look – we'll go out. To the coast. Somewhere we don't have to check the exits or work out if thass the same weirdo we saw two blocks back. Sound good?

ROSEMARY: Pity your bike isn't up to it.

RICHARD: We'll take the wagon. I can drive.

He is holding the bottle of booze. He puts it down.

Okay, Rosie?

ROSEMARY: Fine.

RICHARD: I'm the hysterical one, okay. Let's keep this thing simple.

ROSEMARY: As a matter of fact, my father would have liked you. He'd have taken you for a drink.

RICHARD: No kiddin'.

He exits to the bathroom.

(Off) O man, my fucking boots! Fuck. Two hundred dollars I paid fer these. Fucking shower gel...

She is in control again. She walks to the window, carrying the cup, and looks out, weary.

ROSEMARY: We won, we won, we won.

Good old us.

Noise from outside begins to seep in, till it floods the space, cries of 'Please don't kill your baby' are heard. It is then cut off.

RICHARD: *(Off)* Sonofabitch! ...

ROSEMARY: They're boots, not the Taj Mahal ...

The exit door swings open. A figure enters, dressed in leathers, gun trained on ROSEMARY. RICHARD emerges from the shower, still wearing the towel, laughing, carrying boots and leathers, tipping water from his boots.

RICHARD: *(Off)* We got fucking goldfish back here...!

ROSEMARY: No...

The figure, distracted, fires two shots at RICHARD. He is knocked backwards. As ROSEMARY reacts, the figure turns and fires at her, the shot knocking her to the floor. RICHARD slumps, the figure wheels round again, and fires a fourth shot. ROSEMARY is on the floor, writhing with pain. The figure wheels towards her again, but the gun clicks, and clicks again. A pause. The sound of the shower. Fade lights.

Scene Two

A large attic in a downtown building. A skylight, a desk. There are unpacked boxes containing office gear; telephones, a computer, etc. and downstage, a sleeping bag. Upstage-left, corresponding to the shower room door in the previous scene, a door to a kitchenette is slightly ajar. Likewise, the door to the stairs and landing, stage right. By it, a security intercom unit. ANGELA is sitting on the desk attending a small piece of kit which she is probing with a screwdriver. As the lights come up, the intercom is buzzing.

ANGELA: (*Calling*) Iss open.

She listens. Offstage a door slams. She slips off the desk and unhurriedly puts the bit of kit in the desk drawer, then exits into the kitchenette. JOHN enters from downstairs.

ANGELA: (*Off*) I hope thass not you, Father D.

JOHN: Angela?

Angela returns, carrying a ghetto blaster.

Hi.

ANGELA: Hey John.

Beat.

JOHN: So wass happenin'.

ANGELA: Not much. I didn't even wash my face yet.

Beat.

JOHN: You didn't fix that thing?

ANGELA: Yes I did. It gets pretty quiet up here.

JOHN: More Bobby D huh.

She is plugging the blaster in.

ANGELA: Iss not possible ta have too much Dylan.

These coupla albums anyway. You don't like him?

JOHN: Yeah, I like him. I just heard he backslid.

ANGELA: You heard that too huh.

JOHN: Went back ta bein' Jewish.

ANGELA: Well, he's rewindin' now alright.

You want coffee?

JOHN: Hey let me.

ANGELA: No, I got it.

She exits to the kitchenette. Water running.

JOHN: I got more Dylan if you wanna borrow some.

ANGELA: (*Off*) Thass kind.

I don't really go fer the 'fore an' after stuff.

The buzzer.

ANGELA: You bring someone up with you?

JOHN: Not me.

She leaves the kettle on the desk and calls through the door.

ANGELA: Iss open. Come on up.

Thass next on the list – ah'm gonna have no throat left.

JOHN: Some list.

ANGELA: More you do, more you gotta.

She attends the ghetto blaster. Music in, then down.

ANGELA: Oh Lord.

She turns the music off and stands up. FATHER D enters, labouring.

FATHER D: Oh man. Child, either we get that lift sorted, or I need oxygen on the first floor...

ANGELA: Father D, this is John.

FATHER D: John.

ANGELA: John's the guy from Ohio I was tellin' you about.

JOHN: Dr Price.

FATHER D: Hey John. Ohio's loss our gain, huh.

JOHN: I hope so, Dr Price.

FATHER D: Hey, Father D, Father Dave whatever. I'm gonna have enough of that Reverend Doctor stuff this week. Nice ta see yer, John.

FATHER D: You get those plane tickets ah'm givin' blood for?

ANGELA: I did.

FATHER D: Well praise god fer small mercies.

ANGELA: I gave 'em the guy next door. The courier guy? They'll be at the desk by now.

FATHER D: You get my name put out?

ANGELA: I didn't. I thought, you know, security an' all.

FATHER D: No thass right. Thass right. Well, John.

Looks like you joined us on a auspicious occasion. I'm gonna miss my flight taday.

ANGELA: You still got twenty minutes Father D. I'll
    drive yah.
FATHER D: Woah-woah. I got a cab downstairs took
    more 'n thirty get back over here. Iss okay.
ANGELA: We could phone.
FATHER D: We could try that ...
ANGELA: I got 'em here someplace.
    *JOHN and ANGELA search boxes, FATHER D
    sits heavily.*
FATHER D: Man, iss warm out there. I didn't know
    better, I'd say I got one a my ol' ma's hot flushes
    comin' on.
JOHN: I've got it. Here, Father D.
FATHER D: They left us a socket round here?
ANGELA: Behind you by the door, John. You need the
    number.
FATHER D: You guys done a lot a good work up here.
    Thanks.
    As he punches the numbers.
    I better not be the only one prayin' here.
ANGELA: John lifted most of the stuff last night. Him
    an' the others.
FATHER D: Yeah, I get departures? Internal. Thanks.
ANGELA: Wanna coffee, Father D?
FATHER D: (*No*) Ah uh. Hello, this is Reverend Doctor
    David Price – I gotta reservation today on flight –
    wassa flight number?
ANGELA: VA five somethin' – you won't need that.
FATHER D: Hi – I gotta flight today, the 9.50 to
    Vancouver, I'm runnin' 'bout twenty minutes behind
    schedule. F'I beg real hard, is there a chance a you
    holdin' that flight? Yes sister, I will...
    You guys sleep up here last night?
ANGELA: That was me.
JOHN: I gotta place over at the hostel, coupla blocks
    away. Came over early see what was goin' on.

FATHER D: You know you a brave volunteer Angela,
You coulda had Jean or one a the others stay over
here, keep you company lass night.

ANGELA: I wanted ta get on with some stuff, Father D,
this demo comin' up. 'Sides, I didn't feel I was alone.

FATHER D: Hey, yeah, iss me... No kiddin' – Well
Praise God fer that. Yeah and you...
Even 'fore our prayers are on our tongue the Lord
hears and replies.

ANGELA: They holdin' it?

FATHER D: Delayed forty-five. That gives me juss'
about time ta get back over there.

ANGELA: I'll drive yer, Father D.

FATHER D: No, iss okay, cab's waitin'. Least I hope it
is. It worked John – the prayers of a righteous man
have a powerful effect.

JOHN: Bye, Father D.

FATHER D: You around here some more?

JOHN: I can be, 'less I get some work.

FATHER D: Any spare time you got, we'll use it. Right,
Angela?

ANGELA: I guess so ...

JOHN: Great.

FATHER D: Don't let her work you too hard now. You
hear me, Angela? I sooner have a live sinner than...

FATHER D *and* ANGELA: ... than a dead saint anyday.

ANGELA: You gotta go, Father D.

FATHER D: She knows all my best tunes.
*At the door, he tries the light switch – the light
comes on.*
Oooh wee. I prophecy big bills comin' our way real
soon.

ANGELA: Go.

FATHER D: God bless you both.
FATHER D goes out.

ANGELA: (*Calling*) Father D – you gonna do Mrs
Enright?

FATHER D: (*Off*) I don't think so.

ANGELA: (*Calling*) You should – it always gets 'em.

FATHER D: (*Off*) I'll let you know, child.

> *Pause.*

ANGELA: I won't spoil Ma Enright for yah.

JOHN: No I heard it. Walkin' in the light, Sermons Five through Twelve. Mrs Enright comes up twice, if I recall.

ANGELA: You got all them tapes?

JOHN: Sure.

ANGELA: I guess you gotta be on another planet not ta hear Mrs Enright least once.

Congratulations, John. You passed round one.

JOHN: Yeah?

ANGELA: He always says, worst jokes fer the best people.

> *Pause.*

JOHN: So, is there a plan fer the day?

ANGELA: Truth is John, Father D likes ta have a proper sit-down with all the volunteers 'fore they get too involved. Check out you the kinda person the Lord can use round here.

ANGELA: I don't mean ta be rude or nothin', iss juss the way we do things.

JOHN: Right.

ANGELA: (*Brightly*) You passed round one.

JOHN: Round two's the sit-down, huh.

ANGELA: I hope yer not too disappointed?

JOHN: I'm kinda impatient, I guess.

ANGELA: We all get that.

I guess it wouldn't hurt if you had some coffee.

JOHN: I don't want ta get you inta trouble ...

ANGELA: Iss okay. Some people don't have a godly way seein' things. We have ta be alert and wise.

Father D's real grateful fer all yer help last night.

JOHN: So, Coffee's okay?

ANGELA: I guess.

JOHN: You havin' some?

ANGELA: I'm thirsty.

JOHN: I'll get it.

He plugs in kettle, sorts out mugs on tray etc. She begins to unpack computer stuff.

ANGELA: I ain't use ta anyone pickin' the kettle up round here 'cept me.

JOHN: I gott lotta experience coffee-wise. That n'stamp lickin'. Back home I done coffee makin', stamp lickin', envelope stickin'. I even got ta speak at a rally one time.

ANGELA: You did?

JOHN: Tellin' folks where ta park the pick-ups. Iss real backwoods country up there. Y'know, some of them old guys, they won't use a microphone on account the Lord Jesus never had one. I'm serious. 'Nough ta drive you crazy if you didn't hang on ta God's promise.

ANGELA: You gotta promise from God?

JOHN: Well, kind of. You learn all this technical stuff at college?

ANGELA: I worked in a office fer a while, thass all.

JOHN: Yeah? Where was that?

ANGELA: Up in Selma. Selma Alabama.

JOHN: Selma huh.

ANGELA: Iss juss a li'l place.

JOHN: You never seen Akron, Ohio. I guess we both found our deliverance, hey Angela.

So you gonna show me round this rig sometime?

ANGELA: I would. Like I said John, I can't do that juss yet.

JOHN: Sure. No problem. Here's yer coffee.

ANGELA: Thanks. I wanna make sure iss all up an' runnin' anyway, 'fore I let anyone loose on it. Lass time it crashed, took a week juss puttin' the mailshot back on.

JOHN: Yeah? Big job, huh.

ANGELA: Takes time thass all.

JOHN: One thing th'unborn don't have, right?
How's the coffee?

ANGELA: I've tasted better.

JOHN: I guess experience ain't everythin', right. So,
what else you do fer the unborn? You say there's a
demo comin' up?

ANGELA: We do. I can't talk about it too much.

JOHN: We done whole lot a demos in Akron.

ANGELA: They approve a demos?

JOHN: S'long as they the quiet kind, nobody notices.
Man I got so frustrated. I'm glad I'm outa all that
thinkin'.

ANGELA: Well, you got yer promise from God, right?

JOHN: Yeah right. S'not much. Not enough ta start a
church on. Just that he could use me, y'know. Tell the
truth, fer someone like me, thass quite a lot.

ANGELA: I give you a word advice, John. Fer when you
with Father D. You come on ta him like you a
untalented individual, like you ain't quite what
th'Lord's gonna make you yet, he's gonna give you a
real hard time.

JOHN: Yeah?

ANGELA: I'm talkin' two, maybe three-hour prayer
sessions. All 'bout how you a mighty child a God,
how the devil's this little squitty guy don't hold a
candle. Most folks figure iss best ta make out you got
a real good self image, even if thass not quite the
truth. Know what ah'm sayin'?

JOHN: That obvious huh.

ANGELA: Ah'm juss sayin'.

JOHN: I'll try an' remember that.
Pause.
Angela. Can I ask you a question?

ANGELA: 'Bout the rig?

JOHN: 'Bout Father D.
Beat.

ANGELA: Alright.

JOHN: I'm not quite sure how ta put a question like
this. You ever think Father D's kinda different
from us?

ANGELA: How's that?

JOHN: I don't mean cause he's black ...

ANGELA: I hope not.

JOHN: I don't.

Now I met him, Father D's even more than what
I thought he was. All full a joy an' stuff. He's got all
the words an'... there's so much in him God can use,
fer what we're fightin' for. I'm not juss puttin' a
downer on myself before yer say it. There's things
I can do, I'm not ashamed to admit that. I know cars,
I know guns, I know a few other things. Nothin'
seems ta fit.

I mean I can do other things, I can do posters an'
park pick-ups all day, but thass not really who
I am, Angela. Am I makin' any sense?

ANGELA: You know guns?

JOHN: See god's only spoke ta me twice in my life.
Like twice I know fer sure. One time it was this thing
'bout what I got ta give, that He could use it.
Th'other time was listenin' ta this song. Real old
song, by the Beach Boys, Bee-gees someone like that.
You know the one?

ANGELA: I told yah, I don't listen ta sec'lar music
much.

JOHN: It goes, the pen is mightier than the sword, but
no match fer a gun. Sometimes I'd sit up there in
Akron, tearin' off all these stamps I'm s'posed ta be
stickin' on, thinkin' how every one them is one a the
unborn that'll die taday. I'd juss think a those words.
Do you ever think there'll be a season – I don't
mean now – I mean, the way things are goin', d'you
ever think there'll be a season fer people like us?
People who don't have all the gifts. Gifts a eloquence
and wisdom...

ANGELA: I don't think you got the gift a wisdom, John.

JOHN: Right.

Shit ah'm sorry. I blew it. Lord Jesus I messed up big time.

ANGELA: Iss okay John. I know frustration when I see it. But I know Father D, an' if you knew him like I know him, you'd know he's got the answer fer what you sayin'. He'd never touch stuff like that. He's the most Jesus-like person I ever met, an' if he says violence is wrong, if thass what you talkin' about, thass it. And he's right, y'know, because Jesus, he never went near violence 'cept what was done ta him. Or what he healed up in people.

JOHN: But he got angry, right.

ANGELA: He did...

JOHN: He turned the tables, right?

ANGELA: Thass different. Father D says we can never be that righteous.

JOHN: Not even when we born again?

Pause.

JOHN: Hell you're right. I'm sorry. O Lord, I hardly even got here.

Pause.

JOHN: I'm really sorry.

ANGELA: Thass okay, John.

JOHN: Tell the truth, I bin hangin' around here fer weeks, always figurin' there's somethin' else goin' on, some kinda, higher level. I look at you an' Father D, I know you're special. I always wanted ta be part of somethin' like that.

You're gonna tell Father D now, huh.

Pause.

ANGELA: I don't think I can drink this.

ANGELA takes coffee cups into the back room, then returns.

ANGELA: John.

JOHN: Yeah, iss okay, I gotta get back anyhow. I'm sorry.

ANGELA: Maybe we keep this between us, okay.
Way I figure is, if God wants Father D ta know, he'll
tell him anyway. He prob'ly knows already if he done
his prayin' this mornin'.

JOHN: You mean that?

ANGELA: You gotta see him though, John. Soon as he's
back. You got a number he can call you on?

JOHN: There's a payphone end a tha hall.

ANGELA: I think we better say Thursday. Afternoon
be best.

JOHN: You keep his diary too?

ANGELA: I kinda am his diary. Say two after lunch?

JOHN: Great.

ANGELA: I don't recommend you tell Father D 'bout
this. He's kinda sensitive juss now, everythin' goin'
on an' all.

JOHN: Sure. I appreciate this, Angela. I don't know...

ANGELA: Iss okay John.
I gotta get cleaned up now.

JOHN: Right. Get yer face washed.

ANGELA: I believe God knows how everythin' fits
together. That goes fer us juss like it goes fer the
unborn. He's the only one knows what part goes with
what. We juss need ta be patient an' wait fer salvation.
It'll come.

JOHN: I won't ferget this. I won't ferget Thursday,
neither.

ANGELA: You better not. My policy is, three strikes an'
your out. You two down already.

JOHN: I done two things?

ANGELA: Coffee oughta count double, in my opinion.
He pauses by the door.

JOHN: Thanks Angela. I appreciate this.

ANGELA: You're welcome.
*She smiles. He goes out. She waits until she hears the
slam of the downstairs door. A moment. Going to the desk,*

she pulls open the drawer. After a brief pause, she shuts the drawer, and goes into the backroom. Blackout.

Scene Three

A lecture theatre. A projector screen on which is back-projected a slide of a mock-graveyard – hundreds of small white crosses. A small lectern is being placed in front of the screen. FATHER D, speaks in the near-dark, using a tie-mic.

FATHER D: Can we have the lights up just a little?
The lights begin to come up, and the slide is disturbed.
No, leave that. Thanks.

Jus so I can see who we got here. Thank you.
The slide is repositioned so it can just about be seen on the screen. The lights dip a little and steady. All FATHER D's comments in the scene are now directed out front, though there may be a little 'playing to the wings'. He might also begin speaking when stage staff are still on-stage

You know, when we set out that garden of remembrance you see behind me here – can you see that? There's about five thousand of those little crosses in all. Every one of which represents the life of a child ended in the womb in the United States of America – today. Today. And yesterday, and tomorrow, and the day after. Far as the eye can see. When we set that out, we were told – I have to quote this – we were accused of 'recklessly evoking the imagery of war'.

That's the verdict of one a those independent, impartial journalists we hear so much about – 'recklessly evoking the imagery of war'. It was thought we might upset people who had lost loved ones in the two world wars of this century – some of you might wanna say, the *other* two world wars – by

43

equating those lives which were cut short, with these lives which were cut out. Completely. And literally. I dunno. That's how blind the world has become to its own effect. In our generation.

Well, I've just about finished casting my pearls of wisdom before you guys... 'fore I go I want to finish with a few thoughts about this past year and where it leaves us. And more important than that, to say a few words about the work that is before us.

What a year. Nineteen ninety whatever it is. Could already be two thousand years since Christ walked on this earth, we don't really know. Like those moving walkways at the airport. 'I wonder where this moving pavement *is* they keep telling us about – hey I'm already on it.' That's how time is. Seems to me we are in the last days, whether we like it or not.

What a year. A year of riots, lawlessness and law. Political corruption, wars, rumours of wars, immorality, infidelity, widespread – we may say total – human inadequacy. I include myself in that last one. Inadequacy. The ultimate miracle of God's beloved creation has become unlovely, almost unloveable. Survival of the morally weakest – thass the rule by which the Western world has decided to determine its future. We may feel a good deal, we may worry ourselves to sleep at night. But when it comes to decisive action, we – we close our eyes. Some of you are closin' your eyes right now, I realise that. But we don't have ta be sitting down to do it. Hey, there's a problem.

He drops his head on his chest, makes a snoring noise into the mic.

Y'know when I look around me back home in Pensacola, I don't find this too surprising. Ours is just a sleepy little place. An' Operation Freedom – thass what we call ourselves – Operation Freedom's just same as everything else in our neighbourhood.

You read the paper – *New York Times, Washington Post*
– they make us out ta be real high-tech. Like we been
in the desert practisin' karate with the Colonel hisself.
Tell yer, I come away, someone drives me to the
airport, someone else comes ta wave goodbye, that's
halved our numbers. We got a little ol' lady, name of
Mrs Enright, she's ninety-seven. She answers all our
post. Some of you'll know if you've written to us, she
can't read too well, her typin's pretty bad; I said to
one of our people one day, you think we oughta ask
Mrs Enright step down a little? Are you crazy Dr
Price. See that minibus over there? I says yeah, I see
it. She's the only one knows how ta do the oil change.
Maybe I'm exaggeratin' a little. Her mother's
pretty good.
We may be sleepy, we may be inadequate and we
may feel ourselves to be so, but there's a lot of folks
out there – an' maybe some here tonight – feel
strongly 'bout the holocaust goin' on around them.
Not all of them saved, not all of them. And it's weird,
but these people look to Operation Freedom an' all
the thousands of other, most of them bigger, little
Operations across this country for some kind of lead.
They wanna know what they can do will make a
difference. They wanna know if there is hope in this
war of indiscriminate killing.
We have become a beacon set on a hill. Whether we
like it, or whether we don't.
First thing we can do is pray and pray hard. I don't
remember a time when I felt more in need a prayer,
more hard pressed by the enemy than I do today.
I mean it. But that's not what you're askin', is it.
Least I don't think so.
It's almost a year ago this week since that cosy little
image of ourselves we got in our town was blown
away. See, behind those neat little yards and those
nice shiny cars there's somethin' else going on.

We gotta federal government bankrupt in more ways
than I care ta mention and a state that sits by and
watches thousands of dollars bein' pumped into what
they call family planning. What you know and I
know as genocide.

Our town's bin pretty good at keepin' a leash on
them burger bars. But we still bin' made a service
centre. You get an appointment at any one a the
clinics in our town, they'll give you a take out soon
as whistle. I don't mean ta be flippant. I don't mean ta
be disrespectful, but that's about as much as they
think about a child's life. Somethin' you can keep or
dump, dependin' on your appetite.

'Bout a year ago, some guy went wild with a gun,
shot an abortionist right there in the surgery where
this abortionist performed her works. I believe she
called them terminations. Shot somebody else too.
That tha sort of thing we should be doin', Pastor
Mahoney? Reverend White? Senator Brent? It's a real
question. How do we stop somethin' the state won't
let us stop, but we know is wrong, an' more than
wrong, is evil, when the government won't have it
any other way?

A year ago that question became real for us, and you
all know tha story. There was reporters everywhere,
camera crews all over town, wantin' ta know what
Operation Freedom was gonna do ta bring the culprit
to justice. Did we approve? Had we helped in
planning that hit? As self-proclaimed leader of
Operation Freedom – you hear that? self-proclaimed
leader; they sure spread that impartiality around
don't they. They wanted to know, 'what are you goin'
do about it, Father Dave?' Took them a while ta get
round ta me a course. They had ta question Ma
Enright five hours. Find out her secret cookie recipe.
Now I've bin asked, even here in the last couple of
days ta be real clear on this point so that's what I'm

going ta do. I hope you'll be patient with me and listen carefully to what I say. I told those reporters what I believe is the truth and I'm gonna tell you th'same thing here tonight. It is not possible, it makes no sense, for any organisation that owns the name of Christ and aims ta represent him and his values in the world to set out to achieve the destruction either of the innocent or of the guilty. Do I make myself clear? Do you hear what I'm sayin'? Christ chose the road of sacrifice. When Peter chopped off some guy's ear, Jesus put it back on again. Life is not property. Life cannot be owned. Life belongs only to the maker. This year I suggest we listen to Him. As we get nearer the Day, brothers and sisters, we *have* to listen to Him. Millions, maybe more than millions of innocent lives depend on our obedience. We gotta listen to our Father real good, and that's when we just started. Next we gotta be obedient. Even unto death.

Under the 1993 bill introduced by the government of President George Bush – I know, I know – under the law of this land, mass demonstrations like the ones we embark upon this weekend, are practically, by which I mean *in practice*, illegal. Between we few people here tonight, we could serve, I don't know how many years in jail for what we're going to do. I could get ten years fer askin' you to do it. Between us we may yet serve a millennium. Choose this day – choose this year – whom you will serve. Forsake all others – and I include myself in that – forsake Doctor Price if I take a wrong turn. Our God in heaven'll sort me out. Follow only Him. Above all – as those t-shirts used ta say the kids wore in the eighties – Choose Life. And may that life be the Life that is yours eternally. Amen? Amen. That's all. Pastor Mahoney? Mr Salako, Thank you.
Lights down.

Scene Four

ROSEMARY's office. Rosemary stands with her back to the (outside) door, still wearing her coat. RICHARD manoeuvres his electric wheelchair around the office.

ROSEMARY: What about over here?

RICHARD manoeuvres to the place ROSEMARY is indicating — just in front of the shower room door.

Wait a minute.

She leans over him to open the door. RICHARD looks at her, then without speaking reverses into the shower room. The chair stops, with him out of sight. He moves the chair forward, and appears again on stage. A brief pause.

ROSEMARY: You're not trying.

RICHARD: Fuck trying.

The phone rings.

ROSEMARY: I'm not sure this is a good idea.

ROSEMARY turns and takes her coat off, hanging it on the back of the door. The answering machine cuts in fairly quickly.

RICHARD: This is Rosemary Bright's private line.
I can't get to the phone blah blah blah but if you're phoning me in my professional capacity, I should warn you all my calls are now taped and traced and I love to prosecute.

Beat. He smiles.

ROSEMARY: What does Lefevre say?

RICHARD: Lefevre? Does he have your number?

MALE VOICE: (*On the tape*) Hi there ...

She switches the tape to mute.

ROSEMARY: What are they telling you at the hospital.

RICHARD: Something else I don't recall, doc.
Loss of memory is normal. Feeling pissed off is normal. Be patient, Mr Fiske. Be *a* patient. Most of all, Mr Fiske, be *our* patient. Sign here. What else are they gonna say?

ROSEMARY: What else do they say?

RICHARD: What would they say?

ROSEMARY: What else does Lefevre say?

Beat.

RICHARD: If Dr Death does not record the message, how does she know when to prosecute?

ROSEMARY: It is recording. And don't call me that.

He smiles.

RICHARD: Still got that heavy breather, huh?

She turns off the mute button, but the message has finished. She rewinds. And presses play.

ROSEMARY: They make and cancel appointments. Then phone to tell me how clever they've been. One more life that got away. Things like that.

MALE VOICE: (*On tape*) Hi there Rosemary, this is Ron Bish...

She halts the tape. Pause. She turns it on again, and disappears into the shower room. The same voice is heard on the tape, surprised at first, then droll.

VOICE: (*On tape*) ...op. Are you getting nuisance calls? Listen er, the formal lunch is gonna take place on the 28th of next month. Everyone here's real excited the college board made the appointment, though frankly if they coulda had you full time they'd have been a little happier. I explained you were a woman of strong principle, and for reasons I can't imagine they believed me. Anyway, you should get the official lunch card in a week or two – I just wanna make sure you're polishing that acceptance speech. Any problems, give me a call.

Message ends. RICHARD moves over to the tape, and presses rewind, then play. First message begins.

VOICE: (*On tape*) Rosie, this is Christine Halcutt. We're looking to peg that article on the other one – er, I'm not making much sense. Can you call me, I'm on the mobile. Bye.

Beep

FEMALE VOICE: (*On tape*) Dr Bright, Sian at Welfords. I'll call you.

Beep

MALE VOICE: (*On tape*) Hi there, Rosemary. This is Ron Bishop. Are you getting nuisance calls? Listen er, the formal lunch is gonna take place on the 28th of next month. Everyone here's real excited the college board made the appointment, though frankly if they coulda had you full time they'd have been a little happier. I explained you were a woman of strong principle, and for reasons I can't imagine they believed me. Anyway, you should get the official lunch card in a week or two – I just wanna make sure you're polishing that acceptance speech. Any problems, give me a call.

Following dialogue partly overlaps the above messages.

ROSEMARY: (*Off*) Any wiser?

RICHARD: That's him. That's that fucking heavy breather. You got his home number?

ROSEMARY: (*Off*) Yes.

RICHARD: Now why does that surprise me.

He looks around the room again. Off, we hear the brushing of teeth.

RICHARD: You know in a near-death experience there should be light at the end of the tunnel. No fucking light here.

ROSEMARY: (*Off*) Quieter though.

She returns to the doorway, this time with a hairbrush.

ROSEMARY: Out there anyway.

What did Lefevre say?

RICHARD: Apparently memories are gonna come flooding back. Seems I have the past to look forward to anyway. Meanwhile I get ta pop more pills than Unichem. Satisfied?

Message has ended, tape resets. ROSEMARY keeps brushing her hair.

RICHARD: This room is still the same colour, right?

ROSEMARY: Same room, same colour. You remembered something.

RICHARD: I still go blank on all primary colours, doc – red, mostly.

She pulls the hair from her brush.

ROSEMARY: Like I said, why should I move.

RICHARD: Do you suppose there's an opposite to *déjà vu*? The feeling you haven't been in a place you once knew well? Maybe I'll ask Lefevre next time.

You know if you choose to take other lovers in the light of my incapacitation, I'll understand. Then I'll kill the bastard.

ROSEMARY: He's Ron Bishop and he's the university vice principal. They offered me a post.

She pours herself a drink.

RICHARD: The university principal of vice offered you a job over there. I knew that, huh?

ROSEMARY: *I* don't remember everything. The offer came months ago. I turned him down, he doesn't give up easily, I changed my mind.

RICHARD: We're talking about the job, right.

Beat.

RICHARD: But not full time.

ROSEMARY: I asked for an honorary post. That way I get to choose my hours.

RICHARD: And still work here.

ROSEMARY: I think I should practise what I preach. Can we change the subject?

RICHARD: What subject is that, doc?

ROSEMARY: Richard, I'm sorry things are difficult...

RICHARD: Apology accepted.

Too bad your old man drank himself to death. I could use a drinking pal.

Pause.

ROSEMARY: Richard, did I say forget to say thank you for lunch?

RICHARD: I dunno. Did I tell you I like your hair that way?

ROSEMARY: Yes. Twice.

Beat.

RICHARD: Too busy for academia, huh.

ROSEMARY: Are you offering career advice?

RICHARD: Sounds to me like you got all the 'vice' you need. Thanks fer the flowers, by the way. Nice thought.

ROSEMARY: Fine.

RICHARD: Red roses, then yellow, all the way till last month. Suddenly – red again.

I did decide it was 'cause all the time I was playing Coma, you were out here stitching a sign on sayin': 'Hi, I'm Rosie, the Academic Public Figure Abortionist, shoot me'. But if Ron has been facilitating that explains everything. Red being the colour of guilt an' all.

ROSEMARY: Alright. I confess. We're eloping to Las Vegas. I am too busy for pure academia as it happens. I've discovered there is actually something *as* important as work. The right to do it. So I decided to fight. But back in real life, my clients still need me, so I keep working. A compromise. I actually thought you'd be pleased.

RICHARD: You should see Lefevre. This is classic displacement behaviour.

ROSEMARY: Really? If I'd taken the job you'd say I was selling out.

RICHARD: Classic displacement.

ROSEMARY: As long as it's classic...

RICHARD: You don't believe you got shot for doing a job, or worse, for no reason at all, so the job gets to be a cause. Like when those security guys get killed, their fat wives keep and press the uniform. 'Once they screwed overtime for Group 4, now they're fuckin' heroes.' You got your cause, doc. You're big

news. Every guy woulda shot Lennon, Reagan and
JFK if they had the balls is trackin' Dr Death now.
Bang. Hey now, that wasn't too bad. Let's shoot some
more of these bastards.

ROSEMARY: Lefevre should watch out.

RICHARD: Lefevre only deals with depressives. We're
talking certifiable lunacy.

ROSEMARY: I hardly think aborting the campaign is
an option, do you?

RICHARD: You are not the same as the campaign.

ROSEMARY: Really? I thought that was the problem.

RICHARD: The bad guys shoot you up, the good guys
steal your face. You are Dr Death-wish.

ROSEMARY: I chose this work. And I chose to help
the campaign. We're winning. Okay we still get the
calls, but things are changing. Have changed. If it
can work here...

RICHARD: All you did Rosie, was scare the sane bad
guys back home to the burbs. You're down to the
hardcore now. The guys who don't mind doin' ten
fuckin' years if it means they make a headline. You
don't win a war like this.
Pause.

ROSEMARY: I had thought I might go home.

RICHARD: To England? Well, that's out of range.

ROSEMARY: Scotland. There's a vacancy at St Anne's.
It's a teaching hospital. I'd be near my mother.

RICHARD: The cause should be glad you stayed. I know
I am.

ROSEMARY: What about you? What will you do with
your life?

RICHARD: I think I might be able to sell more
paintings now.

ROSEMARY: I'm being serious.

RICHARD: Could be the career break I'm looking for.
People find cold pizza such a drag.
He shifts the chair forward.

RICHARD: Enjoy your meal.

ROSEMARY: For god sake, Richard.

You'd better go home and rest.

RICHARD: Work calls, huh, away with the patient.

ROSEMARY: 'He was always a bastard, but he never pitied himself.'

RICHARD: What's to pity, doc? I'm differently abled.

Pause.

ROSEMARY: If it makes you feel better, they weren't my roses. I don't do guilt, remember. Maybe it's you who's caught the public eye. Floral fan mail?

RICHARD: Sure. 'Dear Handsome crippled pizzaman.' You suppose Ron could be chasing us both?

ROSEMARY: Possibly. He's fit, forty and has an enormous swimming pool. Surrounded by athletic young males most weekends.

RICHARD: Shit. That lets me out. I could hardly be described as young, hey doc.

Pause.

ROSEMARY: Richard...

RICHARD: Rosemary.

ROSEMARY: Let's not do their job. I'm doing what's right.

RICHARD: Y'know, Lefevre would love this. I'm lyin' here on the floor – he's shown me the photos, right; the Lefevre school of therapy – I'm lyin' here on the floor, and the buzz – all I remember, as a matter of fact – the buzz is great. So good, I don't hear the guy who's shovin' tubes in, tellin' me ta breathe.

ROSEMARY: So, go and breathe.

Pause.

RICHARD: Maybe it's us who's dead.

ROSEMARY: Us.

RICHARD: Richard and Rosie. Do we foot soldiers figure in this at all?

Beat.

ROSEMARY: I don't think *we* are that important. That's not what I meant.

No girl comes through that door without risking her
life. I'm not going to do less. If being Dr Death for a
while helps us win, so be it. It's a price I have to pay.
Beat.

RICHARD: Well, do me a favour, doc. Don't lock the
drawers. Of the desk, I mean. Say your prayers every
night, *always* wear clean panties, leave a contact
number for your next of kin, make a will before it's
too late. Stay lucky. O but I forgot. Dr Deathwish
doesn't do luck either.

ROSEMARY: That reminds me.

RICHARD: Hey I'm the one with the problem, right?
*She takes out a set of keys, unlocks the drawer, takes
out a package, in a plastic bag. She puts it on
the desk.*

ROSEMARY: The police returned this. Deal with it,
would you.
She exits to the bathroom.

RICHARD: Kinda late fer self-defence.
(*To himself*) Hey, look at this. Fucking Ironside.
As ROSEMARY speaks, RICHARD unwraps the gun.

ROSEMARY: (*Off*) I'll be happier when it's gone.
I won't feel the temptation.
Please go, Richard.

RICHARD: Sure. Why not.

ROSEMARY: (*Off*) I'll call you next week.
*She arrives back in the doorway to find RICHARD
has the gun to his head. He pulls the trigger.*

ROSEMARY: Uuuuh ... !
It clicks harmlessly.

RICHARD: Nope. No fucking light. How was that for you?

ROSEMARY: You bastard. Get out. Get fucking out!
*She throws a glass at him – a pathetic gesture to a man
in a wheelchair. A pause.*

RICHARD: You know, a gun is better than a glass. If it's
loaded.
She exits to the bathroom, slamming the door behind her.

Sure.

He tosses the gun on the floor.

(*Calling*) Know what?

No response.

(*To himself*) I don't remember why I came here anyway.

Lights fade.

Scene Five

A basement room, the lay out of which mirrors that of the OF office; exit door stage right, divider door on the upstage wall, stage right. This time the divider door opens into a small, blind cupboard. The room is furnished with a desk/ table, and nothing else. There are no windows in the room, which is lit by a single lightbulb/striplight. The door is reinforced, and lockable. JOHN is alone in the room, sitting on the table with his knees pulled up to his chin. His bag is on the floor, stage right, and ANGELA's sleeping bag is draped over it. The main door opens and ANGELA enters, carrying a blanket and a plate.

ANGELA: This is the best I could find. Plus I thought you might like a san'wich.

She closes the door behind her.

JOHN: You sure this is okay?

ANGELA: I don't see how anyone can argue with hospitality.

Go ahead. I'm fasting.

He bites into the sandwich.

ANGELA: I make a good san'wich, don't I?

I should, I worked in a diner three years.

She sets about moving his bag, laying out the 'bed'.

JOHN: You don't have to do that.

ANGELA: It's okay.

Nice huh.

JOHN: You better tell me where this diner a yours is. I'll book us a table.

ANGELA: I don't think we could drive to Selma. We coulda sorted out somethin' better if youda called us. There's a whole network fer rooms n' stuff. Fix you up with Ma Enright you wan' us too.

JOHN: Thanks.

ANGELA: I can't believe they juss did that to ya, at the hostel.

JOHN: Iss dog eat dog in them places.

ANGELA: We'll fix somethin up. Father D's back tomorrow.

JOHN: Hey, Angela. I want to apologise fer what happened the other day. Shootin' my mouth off. I'm real sorry.

ANGELA: Thass okay John. I told yer, we all get frustrated.

JOHN: I'd feel so bad if I got off on the wrong foot with Father D. He's kind of a hero. We start over?

ANGELA: Sure.

JOHN: I'm John.

ANGELA: Pleased to meet ya, John. I'm Angela.

JOHN: Angela.

ANGELA: Do you know everyone's got another name? Name God gave us when we was knit together in our mother's womb?

JOHN: No I didn't know that.

ANGELA: Angela, thass just a name my ma thought up when she got ta the registry. 'Fore that we all had a name fits juss who we are. You ever hear that?

JOHN: Sounds like it could be true.

ANGELA: I don't know fer certain, I reckon mine is Perpetua.

JOHN: Perpetua. I should know that.

ANGELA: Ain't in the Bible.

JOHN: Wass it mean?

ANGELA: Not juss what it means. How it sounds. S'beautiful. S'not why it fits me, juss sounds like you go on ferever.

JOHN: Per-pet-ua. You're right. It suits.

God tell you what my name is yet?

ANGELA: I asked.

JOHN: Yeah, what d'he say?

ANGELA: (*Shrugs, smiling*) He said iss on a need-ta-know basis.

She searches for a key in a bunch.

We got a lock-in tonight, I tell yer that?

JOHN: No.

ANGELA: We always have a lock-in when Father D's away. More preachers get killed on the road than any other way.

JOHN: 'Part from alcohol, right.

ANGELA: I'm talkin' about preachers, not priests. Father D's flyin', but iss the same principle. There's a whole gang prayin' on the first floor upstairs. I was gonna say prayin' up a storm, but they prayin' the storm away I guess.

JOHN: You gonna join 'em?

ANGELA: I don't think so. There's things I gotta do tonight.

We got work to do, boy.

JOHN: I can help?

ANGELA: Since you taken up residence... I can't get the door open.

She is trying to open the cupboard door. John takes over.

ANGELA: I hope my ham an' mustard's strengthened you up some.

He succeeds, then hands back the key.

JOHN: It was loose.

ANGELA: You rather be prayin'?

JOHN: No. I'm fine here.

ANGELA: I ain't one a them long-distance prayers neither.

She goes in and starts passing out boxes.

JOHN: We playin' guess the box, huh.

ANGELA: Iss not really a game. You seen these didn't
yer?

JOHN: Sure.

*JOHN picks a completed 'foetus' icon from a box. It consists
of a baby doll, minus a limb or two, covered with what
appears to be blood, and stuck on a short pole.*

ANGELA: We call them 'Legion of the Lost'. 'Fore these
all we had was cardboard gravestones and 'Please
don't kill your baby'. I told 'em, we live in a visual
age, we gotta be visual. Here.

*She passes him a 'fresh' baby doll – he holds one in
each hand.*

JOHN: I never imagined people makin' these things.

ANGELA: They don't make themselves. Guess thass the
point.

Don't worry, I won't tell the guys I seen you holdin'
that thing.

JOHN: What do I do?

ANGELA: Not much to it. There should be a hammer
here someplace.

*ANGELA fishes in the boxes till she finds a hammer.
JOHN stares at the baby doll in his hands.*

ANGELA: Okay. You ready fer this?

JOHN: Sure.

ANGELA: Here's how okay. Take one of they arms or
legs off – like that. There's a knife in the box here, if
it won't come off easy. Then you cut a hole in the
back part, where it's soft. Not too big, or it's gonna
wobble. Then you push one a these staves in the hole,
force it right the way up. I usually put a nail in.
There's a few in the box there. Some's rusty, but thass
okay. Hammer it so's it's caught nice and firm. Thass
all. Then you pass it on to me, an' I do the rest.

JOHN: How many?

ANGELA: 'Bout a dozen's plenty. We ain't aimin' fer
actual fact.

Pause.

ANGELA: S'okay, John, we got all night.

JOHN begins to work with the knife, making a hole in the doll's back. ANGELA sits on the table, watching.

JOHN: Where d'you get all these in the first place?

ANGELA: Folks donate 'em mostly. Plus we trawl the car boots.

Pause.

ANGELA: Is there a church you bin goin' to down here, John?

JOHN: Town centre place mostly, First Pentacostal.

ANGELA: Big one, huh.

JOHN: They get about two thousand.

ANGELA: They got close circuit?

JOHN: Sure.

ANGELA: Big cars, smart clothes. Li'l guy in a flashy suit tellin' you all vote Republican?

JOHN: (*Smiling*) You got it. 'Fore that I was with the brothers in Akron. That was real small, couple a hundred maybe.

ANGELA: You call couple a hundred small?

JOHN: Yeah, but it was friendly. My folks were there so it was kinda natural.

JOHN: How 'bout your folks?

ANGELA: Father D is my family just about. Mama died in a road crash.

JOHN: I'm sorry.

ANGELA: I don't think the truck knew much about it.

JOHN: No really, I'm sorry.

ANGELA: Thanks.

They say she meant to do it.

'Not your fault. Things happen.'

Can I take a look at that?

He passes her the doll.

ANGELA: Thass good.

ANGELA blows at the edges of the hole.

Needs a new blade. Gotta clean the edges off neat or it looks a mess.

She takes the knife and goes to the desk. Opening the drawer she takes out a small packet and screwdriver and sets about fitting a new blade to the knife.

JOHN: So, you got a dad up there in Selma?

ANGELA: I do, but I don't see him. I was born in Mobile. S'only 'bout hundred miles from here. I don't intend to go back real soon.

JOHN: The church is your family, huh.

ANGELA: Sure was, Father D led us out when the devil got his claws in.

Try that.

I like it better now anyhow. More focus.

There's more nails if you need 'em.

JOHN: I'm fine. Yep, that's a whole lot better.

He clamps a nail between his lips, and forces a stave into the hole. He is becoming more absorbed by the job now, and she watches him work. He tamps the stave down, then picks up the hammer and positions the nail to finish off.

JOHN: Father Dave's flying back tonight, right?

ANGELA: Ah huh.

He hammers the nail through the baby's back.

JOHN: And ol' Angela's in charge while he's gone.

ANGELA: I am down here, I guess.

JOHN: What's that like?

ANGELA: You done?

JOHN: I think so.

He blows bits away and passes it over.

ANGELA: Not bad. Okay baby, here it comes.

She produces a plastic bottle of red paint.

ANGELA: Don't worry, iss only paint.

Hold it still.

She squirts the paint onto the doll, while he holds it.

JOHN: That's bad.

ANGELA: Reminds me a doin' strawberry sauce at
    the diner.

    Okay I'll take it.

    *She exchanges the paint for the icon, and twists and turns
    the doll to make the paint run down in the desired manner.*

JOHN: I bet you was good.

ANGELA: I don't like ta boast.

JOHN: Better than office work, huh?

ANGELA: Well. You meet people in a diner.

    Here, your turn.

    She passes the icon over, and watches the doll being turned.

ANGELA: You don't wanna know what I did after that.

    Needs a bit more...

    She squirts more paint.

ANGELA: Turn it John. Iss comin' off!

JOHN: I got it.

ANGELA: Thass better. Hey, you're a natural.

JOHN: Yes ma'am. I can see why you like this sport.

    Office worker, waitress, sculptress. What else you got
    t'offer the workplace, Miss Angela?

ANGELA: Put it in here okay.

    *She flips the box over onto its side, so the holes punched in
    the side are uppermost.*

JOHN: You got this all organised, don't yer?

    He puts the end of the stave into the hole.

ANGELA: I sure do. You don't, you got mess all over.

JOHN: So er, what else you do?

ANGELA: I was a cleaner.

JOHN: Yeah? No shame in that. My ma was a cleaner all
    her life.

ANGELA: What she clean?

JOHN: Offices and stuff. Dad said she woulda done the
    hospital if they'd a let her.

    She died when I was ten. Now I juss got my step ma,
    live an naggin'.

    'Nother one?

    JOHN starts on another doll.

JOHN: How 'bout you?

ANGELA: I was fifteen. Lived with gran till she died, then I kinda took off.

JOHN: I meant cleanin'. What kinda stuff you do?

ANGELA: All kinds.

What you do fer work in Ohio? Juss stamp lickin'?

JOHN: I done 'bout a hundred things, after college.

ANGELA: Dropped out, huh.

JOHN: I done farm work first off, drove my uncle's truck fer a while. Polished cars, then I got moved ta forecourt.

ANGELA: You done forecourt?

JOHN: Why not.

ANGELA: I clean your win'shield, ma'am?

JOHN: I change your oil ma'am? I charged a dollar a time fer a win'shield.

ANGELA: You charged a dollar a time fer a win'shield?

JOHN: Thass me.

ANGELA: That where you learned guns, huh. Stand and deliver.

JOHN: Not really. I helped out with my Uncle's firin' range. Handled everythin' from small arms ta huntin' rifles.

ANGELA: You done 'splosives?

JOHN: Not me. Hey, I learned my lesson. I know none a that stuff's on the menu.

ANGELA: Thass good. We gotta do more work, talk less.

JOHN: Yes ma'am.

ANGELA: C'mon boo boo, we gotta move move move, wi' Ol Officer Dibble comin' back here.

JOHN: Minnie Mouse right?

ANGELA: Careful boy, you wanna keep this job.

JOHN: You know if there's a legion, that means we gotta do a thousand a these things.

ANGELA: Thass okay John, you got all night.

He hammers in a nail. She picks up one of the icons.

JOHN: How long they take ta dry?

ANGELA: Iss warm, it won't take long.

Pause.

ANGELA: You know when I was a kid, mama bought me this book. Where you wet the pages with water and the colour comes out?

JOHN: Magic painting.

ANGELA: Magic painting. There was this one picture, you had ta join the dots first, 'fore you got ta paint. I done it over an' over till the page got so wet it tore apart. This Roman soldier holdin' up this big yella eagle, gold I suppose it was. Looked like a... like a...

JOHN: Standard?

ANGELA: Looked so powerful. I used ta look in its eye and shake. Thass the feelin' I get with these things. Like there's a power in them. God's power I guess. Power of the unborn.

JOHN: Thass how it works, huh.

ANGELA: It ain't that simple. Juss sayin' how it makes me feel.
Be encouraged, John. Yer not the only one talks junk round here.

JOHN: You gonna do the paint on this one?

ANGELA: Your turn, win'shield boy.

JOHN: Okay, I hope I do it good.

Pause.

ANGELA: You know those guys shoot abortionists like you were sayin'? They reckon they save a thousand babies a time.

JOHN: Ah huh.

ANGELA: There was this Islamic woman I read about, one of those tiger people? Blew herself ta pieces. Kinda tragic, I think. She lays her life down at this rally – only kills 'bout thirty or forty. She should done it inside I guess. Weird huh, doin' it outside.

JOHN: Yeah, that is weird.

Pause.

ANGELA: Someone did a shootin' up at May Lake, you hear?

JOHN: Wassat?

ANGELA: Somebody got shot. Real near.

JOHN: Yeah, I heard that. That the one with the pizza guy?

ANGELA: He calls hisself an artist.

JOHN: He a friend a yours?

ANGELA: My bosses boyfriend, thass all.

JOHN: At the diner right.

ANGELA: You don't listen, John. I'm talkin' about the clinic now.

JOHN: Clinic? You worked at May Lake?
Father D know 'bout this?

ANGELA: It was Father D's idea, sort of. I seen this job come up, he said go for it. She was real nice, the boss I had. Always smiled at yer, said good mornin' like them English people do. Real Angel of Light, I guess. One day I took this stuff out to the yard, I seen these yellow bags out there – you know, th'sort they put sharps in? There was all these legs an' arms, all higgledy piggeldy. Like a bag a pieces.

JOHN: What you do?

ANGELA: What?

JOHN: What you do when you found that stuff.

ANGELA: I don't think Father D knew what we was gonna do exac'ly, big splash in the papers or somethin'. I took my camera next day, but I never seen nothin'. Thass how clever they are. Next thing one a these crazies breaks in to the clinic, tries ta kill Dr Bright.

JOHN: Shit. Thass how it happened, huh.

ANGELA: They were fornicatin', him an' her. You must a heard 'bout it.

JOHN: I heard somethin'. They didn't catch him.

ANGELA: They didn't. Hard ta respect someone like that, huh. Someone can do that an' walk away, like they ashamed a what they done. Fella on the net said they shoulda bin proud doin' a act of justifiable homicide. Only it wasn't homicide, 'cause she never died. They never knew guns well enough, I guess.

Dr Bright's on the tv all the time now. You seen her?

JOHN: Sure.

ANGELA: I heard her again th'other day. Talkin' 'bout how a unwanted pregnancy's like a li'l bomb tickin' away inside a person. I wish I'd made a tape fer Father D. when I heard it.

JOHN: So nobody questioned you, hey Angela, 'bout the shoot?

ANGELA: Police tried. I let 'em think I's a white trash southern kid, don't know what day it is. Act like you dumb, they don't press too hard. I left the clinic a few weeks after that. Father D said let 'em think the trauma got me. I ain't bin back since thass fer sure. I'm not sure I could go in there again. Not seein' what I seen. In the yard.

Iss true what them videos say, yer know. They ain't juss killin' the unborn in them places. They killin' mankind.

JOHN realises he's spilling the paint.

JOHN: Shit!!

ANGELA: So okay, I got it.

JOHN: Sorry.

ANGELA: Lord never holds yer sins against yer. Here.

JOHN: Thanks.

He takes the cloth from her, and wipes himself.

ANGELA: If I needed help John, with a problem I had, you'd help me right?

JOHN: Sure. Like what?

ANGELA: I don't know exac'ly. If I do, I'll tell yer.

Lord always gives a person a second chance, right.

JOHN: Thanks.

ANGELA: I don't know what you're wipin' your hands for anyway. We gotta whole lot more ta do here tonight.

JOHN: Yes ma'am.

He picks up and begins again. A pause. She sits on the table behind him, as before.

ANGELA: You gotta a favourite vision of heaven, Mr Doll-Maker?

JOHN: Yes ma'am. Heaven means no work and great money. Or no money and great work, I don't mind which. Anythin' don't leave yer bored, broken or broke's okay with me.

ANGELA: Mine's the banquet. I shouldn't talk about this when I'm fastin'. They got the choicest fruits of every kind. We all gonna sit down – unborn, us, everyone. We'll eat whatever the Lord gives. You know what I'm fixed on?

Chicken pie, gravy, an a side dish of french fries. I know thass cheap, but I like it. After that I'm gonna have pecan ice cream and bottomless coffee. Last, you get one a them big ol' peaches with the sun still on it. That diner I worked at? We done peaches covered in real thick chocolate. Used ta call them granny fruit. Kinda warm, furry n' sweet, all at the same time. People used ta taste that chocolate, they'd think they already in heaven.

Sometimes you want somethin' so bad, it doesn't matter what you get – all tastes of dirt.

Pause. She slips off the table, walks to the door, puts her hand flat against it, as if feeling for warmth. She then walks to the bedding, and picks up the blanket.

John.

You wanna touch me, thass okay.

Pause lights fade.

End of Part One

PART TWO

Scene Six

The basement, as before. Early morning. Downstage from the table, the upturned box into which ANGELA was putting the 'legionaires' at the close of Part One now contains over a dozen 'babies', so that it resembles a many-headed monster – or worse, the sort of thing monsters eat at parties. JOHN is turning over his gear, not yet in panic.

Offstage, the sound of a tea tray, followed by a key turning in the lock of the door. Pause.

The door is bumped open. FATHER D enters with the tray.

FATHER D: Room service.

He kicks the door shut behind him.

This is your wake-up call. I hope I'm not too early, John.

JOHN: No, that's fine.

FATHER D: Heard about your situation. Angela take care of you alright?

JOHN: Yeah. Great.

FATHER D: Take your time, it's okay. I'm gonna have some a this coffee myself. I musta inadvertantly crossed a date line or somethin' – I don't know whether it's mornin', night, or Thanksgiving back here. Sleep okay?

JOHN: Yeah, I slept great.

FATHER D: Got the right idea, keepin' yer clothes on. I imagine it gets real cold down here. Post. Guy brought it round from the hostel for yer.

JOHN: Yeah? That's kind.

FATHER D: Lemic, huh. That's er what, a Polish name?

JOHN: Ukrainian.

FATHER D: Ukraine. Right.

So what you make of our little set-up down here, John? Angela tells me you done a few campaigns yerself up there in Ohio.

JOHN: That's right.

FATHER D: You're not plannin' on going up there again, are yer? Not full-time?

JOHN: I'm not sure yet, Dr Price. Depends what work I got. I only bin here a few weeks.

FATHER D: So long as you're here we'll make good use of you.

JOHN: Great.

FATHER D: Take yer time gettin' ta know us, John. I know juss what iss like bein' a square peg in a round hole. Oohwee, I was a hot head in my college days. You know, all the other guys juss had ta be nicely spoken, clean cut-types. Only guy went out of his way to help me was a guy named Paul Ablett. Came from Ohio. I wasn't open to much help at the time. Kinda proud I guess. One time I was so discouraged, I was thinkin' I'd give it all up, go some place nobody talked the English language n' wouldn't know what a hick I was. Paul Ablett, he came round, got on his knees, prayed a solid hour the Lord would meet my need.

JOHN: Sounds like a good friend.

FATHER D: Yeah he was. You ever meet Pastor Ablett up there in Akron, John?

JOHN: No I didn't.

FATHER D: Yeah he er, he moved on a while back. What them Salvationists call promoted to glory. I like that.

JOHN: It's a honour for me ta meet you, Doctor Price.

FATHER D: Well, thass nice of you ta say so, John. You want some more a this coffee?

JOHN: No, I'm fine.

FATHER D: Boy this conference practically wore me out. I mean it's great, seein' them folks from all over. Some a the things I heard, man, they blew me away. You heard the latest thing in California? They playin' classical music to unborn children from two months old. California. Same place most a these pro-choicers hang out. How about that, John. A child in the womb can enjoy classical music from eight weeks, but can't feel pain at twenty-eight. Then you got Chicago on the other side. Coupla months ago, a pregnant woman gets raped, loses her child. Them feminists – them same Chicago feminists what say a foetus ain't a human till iss on the outside – fella told me they pressin' fer a charge a homicide 'gainst this rapist. Lies, deception and delusion. I guess we shouldn't be surprised. Bible tells us the heart of man inches always t'ward evil. Our generation took the devil fer a father, an' them things you made down here are his seed. We can't rest till we got him right out of our national life.

(*Laughing*) There I go again. Preachin' to the converted.

JOHN: You look tired, Doctor Price.

FATHER D: Yeah I am tired. My mouth's bin goin' off like a pike outa water these past few days. Maybe I'll get some sleep an' calm down a little.

FATHER D begins to chuckle to himself.

JOHN: What's funny?

FATHER D: I was juss thinkin'. Man, they had us doin' some crazy stuff on this conference.

JOHN: Yeah?

FATHER D: Sure did. Security. That seems ta be the buzzword. You know they had us trainin' how ta do a body frisk. Like at the airport an' stuff? Help us keep out the crazies.

You wanna see how it's done?

JOHN: Sure.

FATHER D: Come on, get up I'll show yer. You gotta lean on the table there... Hey wait a minute, we need a offensive weapon of some sort. Less you already got one.

JOHN: Knife do?

FATHER D: Yeah that'd be great.

John opens the drawer of the desk, takes out the knife, last seen in scene five.

FATHER D: Okay I'll turn around here – you hide that thing on you someplace. Okay? You done that?

JOHN: One minute. Okay.

John has put the knife flat in his shoe.

FATHER D: Lean against the table there, spread out. Okay, here we go. Start at the top, guns an' stuff usually be in a holster up here, knives along the arms. Nope. Next you do the trunk. They say nobody's gonna put a knife near their abdomen, but a gun's lethal just about wherever, so it could turn up anywhere... nope again. You're good. Now the legs, taking special care at the ankles, sides and back. Guess I didn't pay as much attention as I thought.

JOHN kicks off his shoe, takes out the knife and hands it over.

JOHN: I cheated, Father D.

FATHER D: You one step ahead a the game, John.

JOHN: My dad was in army security. He taught me a few tricks.

FATHER D: Why you son of a gun.

JOHN: I should a told yer.

FATHER D: Well, no that's smart. You know, come ta think of it, that's proved something to me. You search a person an' you don't find, you likely trust that person more 'n you would trust 'em if you didn't do the search in the first place. But if you just a amateur like us guys, you could make a big mistake that way. Miss the gun, knife whatever, you turn your back once too often, iss all over.

JOHN: Guess you gotta practice so you don't miss, thass all.

FATHER D: Yeah, maybe you're right. Maybe we should frisk each other every day from now on, hey John. Get the practice.

JOHN: Yeah why not.

Pause.

FATHER D: You an army boy like yer dad, huh.

JOHN: No sir, I didn't join. I couldn't reconcile fightin' with my Christian beliefs at that time.

FATHER D: Son of mine went in the army. Angela tell yer? Went home in the Gulf. 'Bout your age I guess. What are you, twenty-three, twenty-four?

JOHN: I'm twenty-five.

FATHER D: My Laurie gave his life fighting fer the Muslims. You know how many US boys died in his war, total? One hundred and twenty-four. This boy of mine just had ta be one of 'em. Then I tell myself thirty-three million American children got killed inside their mother's womb since '73, the Roe v Wade judgement. Thirty-three million. More than five times what happened in the death camps, never mind the Gulf. Last time I saw my boy he was lyin' in one a them bags like the ones they throw out a some a these clinics. Only, when those clinics throw 'em out, there's thirty to a bag. Day in, day out. An' nobody ever said a soldier was innocent, did they.

Pause.

JOHN: I'm sorry to hear about your son, Dr Price.

FATHER D: Well, there's gonna be no grievin' in heaven. I guess we gotta get it all done down here.

A brief pause. FATHER D laughs.

Hey, I'm sorry John. I'm startin' ta sound like one a them sad ol' Testament prophets a doom. So, what are you gonna ta do with yourself this week, John?

JOHN: Well, I'd like ta help out if I could.

FATHER D: Angela tell you what we got goin' on here?

JOHN: She said there was somethin'. Wouldn't tell me what. Sounds kinda hush hush.

FATHER D starts putting boxes etc. back in the cupboard.

FATHER D: Yeah, I think ol' Angela'd fit in real well with these conference guys. She show you round that computer a hers she got up there?

JOHN: Not yet.

FATHER D: Tells me you can get just about any kind of information you want on that internet. Thing I like is linkin' up with other guys, coordinating stuff. I think it's Angela's ambition I never go away on conference again. Sit up there, let the ol' fingers do the talkin'. Suits me okay, you gotta struggle like this, you gotta struggle full time.

JOHN: Mrs Price must be real understanding, Father D, you givin' yourself to the cause so much. I'd a thought.

FATHER D: Well, no John, Mrs Price, she er, she passed on pretty soon after Laurie. 'Sides, we both know who the real worker is round here. I'm not supposed ta let on 'bout this, but Angela, she's gonna take a bus load a girls all the way over ta Jacksonville, stand outside the clinic there, give a silent witness of a kind. Quite a different kind, from what I hear.

JOHN: Sounds good.

FATHER D: It should be. Power's not in the parts but in the whole. Right across the country. Coast ta coast and top ta toe. We do our bit, everyone does theirs, gonna make quite a splash. You and me, John, we're on back up. We gonna be back here on our knees. Don't worry, son. We won't be intercedin' the whole time. I got one a two ideas might help us pass the time down here. You er, you gonna eat that toast?

JOHN: I don't eat much in the mornings, Dr Price.

FATHER D: Well I envy you that. Mornin' right?

He eats.

73

FATHER D: So, if your ol' man's from the Ukraine, that
 makes him what over there? A Baptist? Cath'lic?

JOHN: Orthodox.

FATHER D: Orthodox, right. That be Russian
 Orthodox?

JOHN: Ukrainian.

FATHER D: Right yeah, you told me. Okay, I geddit.
 Ukraine.

JOHN: You know I have some computer skills myself,
 Dr Price. I was tellin' Angela...

FATHER D: Yeah? They could come in useful, John, we
 get this demo over.

JOHN: Great.

 So, this nationwide network, that's a regular thing?

FATHER D: We hope it will be. Thass the trouble when
 people lost all faith in government, I tell yer – gets
 hard ta organise squit. Always some brother takin' on
 'bout how we a shadow fer the One World Regime.
 We workin' on it though.

JOHN: You know I really mean it, 'bout what a privilege
 it is to meet you after all...
 Offstage, keys. The door opens.

FATHER D: Hey, talk a the Angel. Now you gotta get
 an eyeful a this. This here's one special lady.
 *ANGELA enters, dramatically transformed. She wears a
 flowing maternity dress, and appears to be pregnant.
 JOHN is dumbstruck.*

FATHER D: Change from all those negative images we
 get stuck with, hey John. Life and life abundant.
 You gonna give us a whirl there Angela?

ANGELA: Father D. I'm Perpetua now.

FATHER D: Hey, I'm sorry. Thass a great name, isn't it?
 And motherhood should be a perpetual thing; thass
 what we tryin' ta protect, right John.

JOHN: Right.

ANGELA: What you guys doin down here?

FATHER D: I juss bin runnin' John through some a the security stuff we done at the meet. You know I like this guy. I think maybe he's okay. Hey, I should know, I frisked him top ta bottom, couldn't find a thing on him.

ANGELA: I'm glad.

FATHER D: I tell yer, she worries...

ANGELA: We had a fax come through upstairs, Father D.

FATHER D: Yeah? A fax huh. Great thing 'bout technology John – bills come thick an' fast.

ANGELA: I think iss a donation. I thought I should leave it for yah.

FATHER D: Sounds like my kinda tune. You know Angela's got five or six of the girls fetched out like this...

JOHN: Great.

ANGELA: Father D...

FATHER D: I'm afraid ol' blabbermouth already blew your secret, child. I told John how our guys in Jacksonville gonna get a real surprise this morning. Know what? These girls get stopped fer speedin', all they gotta say is they on their way ta Jacksonville General!

You gonna give us a turn there, Angela?

ANGELA: I don't think I want to.

FATHER D: Hey come on child, she looks good, don't she?

JOHN: She does.

ANGELA turns round slowly and fairly gracefully – an eery moment.

ANGELA: Think it looks real?

FATHER D: I'd say it suits yer real good. What do you say, John?

JOHN: It's great.

FATHER D: Only person gonna get past you kids into that clinic today is a blindman.

JOHN: That's right.

Pause.

FATHER D: Listen, there's something I wanna share with you, John, while these girls are off doin' their stuff. I'm gonna get that fax, let you have a few moments. I'll be right back.

ANGELA: You leave the door open, Father D.

FATHER D: Sure, child.

You better not go 'fore I said goodbye though.

ANGELA: I won't.

FATHER D exits. A pause.

JOHN: This the big idea?

ANGELA: You don't like it?

JOHN: What's goin' on?

ANGELA: Nothin'. We goin' over ta Jacksonville like Father D said. You sore I didn't tell yer?

JOHN: What's the fax?

ANGELA: He likes gettin' em. Makes him feel we're cuttin' edge.

JOHN: You tell him?

ANGELA: Tell him what, John?

Beat.

ANGELA: I don't think we should discourage everyone with what we done together. We got carried away, thass all.

JOHN: You take somethin' from my bag, Angela?

ANGELA: I took yah gun.

She finds it and hands it over.

I thought I should move it, 'case Father D came down. Lucky I did.

He checks the magazine/chamber.

I left those upstairs. You should be pleased, y'know, I managed not ta shoot myself, takin' 'em out.

JOHN: You think I'm one a them crazies now?

ANGELA: I wouldn't give yer gun back if I thought that. 'Sides Father Dave checked you out, so, no John, I don't think so.

First time we ever strung it together over twenty-four
states. Father Dave's worried they gonna get ahead of
us, nip it in the bud.

JOHN: Who's they?

ANGELA: Police. FBI. The crazies – anyone of 'em
could mess it up. I figure Father D gonna freak he
seen that thing in here.

JOHN: You took my gun to protect me?

ANGELA: You don't need protectin' from Father D.
Everybody here likes you John, but I couldn't explain
the gun, 'cept by sayin you was a crazy. He'd call the
whole thing off.

JOHN: What else d'you find?

Beat.

ANGELA: I found some rubbers a bit late.

Beat.

JOHN: I told you I could handle a gun, Angela.

ANGELA: You didn't tell me you had one, right. I think
you gotta trust people a li'l bit more. Maybe trust
God a little.

JOHN: What about this thing you said I could help
with?

ANGELA: That didn't work out.

JOHN: Since last night?

ANGELA: I think Father D's right. Iss only sacrifice we
got left now. I don't expect you ta understand right
now. There's a lot going on here, John. You sit this
out, you're time'll come. You gotta be patient, you
wanna be involved.

JOHN: An' what if I was a crazy? You gonna leave me
down here with Father D?

ANGELA: You're not a crazy. I know that.
I wasn't sure about this dress. Took me long time
choosin', seein' I couldn't try it on.
You gonna hide that thing?
Beat. He does so.

ANGELA: I think there should always be someone to
protect a child. Grown-ups declare war on children,
there's not much hope.

*FATHER D returns, carrying a portable television set,
and a carrier bag.*

FATHER D: I'm back. They all waitin' upstairs for ya
child. You better get hot-foot up there. Oohweee.

He puts tv down.

ANGELA: Bye, Father D.

FATHER D: I could sure use one a them hugs a yours.

ANGELA: Not now, Father D. I'm feelin' kinda shook up.

FATHER D: Iss gonna be fine, Angela. Y'know
I should be the one worried. I never been a
grandaddy before. God bless you child.

He moves to embrace her. She flinches.

Wow, you are tense.

ANGELA: I love you, Father D.

*She lets him kiss her on the forehead. He is a mite
emotional.*

FATHER D: Th'Lord bless you child. S'gonna be okay.

ANGELA: You say the whole thing for me?

FATHER D: Th' Lord Bless you and keep you, the
Lord make his face ta shine upon you. The Lord lift
up the light of his countenance upon you and give
you his peace. Amen. We prayin' for you, Angela.

ANGELA: Bye, John. Try and think good thoughts about
me, okay?

Take care, Father D.

FATHER D: Don't you worry about us now.

She exits.

Gets me every time those kids go out. I say kids.
Some a them kids are grandparents themselves.
I hope you don't mind me bringin' this down here,
John. I thought we might get our prayin' in 'afore
lunch. Find ourseles all done 'fore the ball game.

*The sound of a key turning in the lock of the door. FATHER
D laughs.*

FATHER D: She's not takin' any chances with us, is she. You like baseball, John?
Blackout.

Scene Seven

The common room. Raucous cheering, banging of tables etc. as ROSEMARY arrives at the lectern. She waits for silence.

ROSEMARY: Three hundred and eighty-five cases of stalking. Forty-five of burglary. Just two kidnappings. Death threats are healthy – two hundred and ninety. One hundred and four cases of assault and battery, seven hundred and twelve of vandalism, three hundred and fifty five of invasion, arson – one hundred and fifty cases. Attempted murders fifteen, actual murders, six. Or is it seven now? You'll forgive me, Chancellor, if my data is a little dusty. I'm rather new to the research game. What a lot the Pro-Life lobby has achieved in the last decade. No cases of paralysis listed – so apparently that doesn't count. Also since 1977, countless numbers of women browbeaten, accosted, and petrified, by people who wish to dictate what a woman may, or may not do with her unwanted pregnancy. As we know, in Brazil, street children often reach the age of three or five, before they're shot. Neglected by the families who haven't the money to feed them, much less the emotional resources to love them, after their three or five – or even nine – loveless years, they're swept from the street like vermin.
The Catholic church quite rightly condemns this murder. Just as it condemns the parents when they try to use contraception. And then condemns the termination of pregnancies thus conceived. Suffer the children is, I believe, the phrase.
I digress. Who do we have here? An off-duty policeman, a nurse, a doctor – well they don't really

count. A bodyguard, ditto. A receptionist, two
receptionists, another doctor. The last dying from a
sniper's bullet, in front of his two small children.
They watched, so the report says, as their father died,
almost instantly, from his wounds. So important to
respect the sanctity of human life.
In the face of all this, in one college at least,
members of the senior common room gather to
welcome to their ranks a survivor. A warm welcome,
very much appreciated. But a welcome into what?
Not, I'm sure Chancellor, a welcome into the safe,
musty life of the intellectual. That myth is long dead.
So I'm told. Today's academic may be a star in the
intellectual firmament, but her feet are firmly planted
in the muck and mire of corporate-sponsored
research.
For that reason too, it can't have been an easy
decision to make, to honour me in this way, so
I salute you. But at the risk of ruining what promises
to be an excellent lunch – I come to offer you, my
new colleagues, and students, a warning. What used
to be called in more innocent days, a call to arms.
You see, Chancellor, outside these hallowed and,
I find, quite intimidating walls, a war has been
declared. And minds as fine as ours, as fine as yours,
are being conscripted. It's you who are Wanted. To
reason, to argue, to present the case for a way of
thinking and a kind of society so – moral – their
crack troops will approach a confused, pregnant girl,
hoping merely to enquire about a termination, and
shove the remains of dead foetus under her nose.
Wrapped in newspaper. This happened a few weeks
ago, where a colleague of mine practises.
These same crack troops will happily pour gasoline
through the broken window of a clinic, and burn
anything, or anyone, inside. In defence of the
defenceless.

As I myself know, these same freedom fighters will gladly take a gun and shoot the legs of a man whose only crime is to know someone who works at such a clinic, who dares to call herself an abortionist. These are the people who wish to enlist you. And I am not ashamed to say, today, that I want your mind, instead. Not for a narrow cause. I want the minds of this faculty – the faculty I join – to serve a different – more demanding society. More intellectually demanding certainly. But not just that. A complicated society, a society with difficult choices to make, a society with alas no time for mealy mouthed, ivory tower, neutrality. A society which knows it has huge choices to make – in the area of genetics for instance, choices which frankly make the appalling decisions faced by some young women today seem comically straightforward, even simple. Now, obviously, if you are going to struggle for a new society, you will need tools – weapons. Don't worry. It's the Chancellor's job to make sure you have them. In fact they should be found lying around any self-respecting campus, even here in the South. The ability to think, to begin with: to decide, to reason, to marshal arguments, to debate, to analyse statistics, to form and present a view. To commit. Ah, that word. No sitting on the fence there. And then you will need some courage. The determination to be a citizen, and not just a subject, of your country. But wait – is there not a third alternative? A third way between these competing societies? Actually, yes. You can carry on, quietly pursuing your chosen discipline, your sporting goals, your social life, your dreams of excellence, this war will rage quite well without help from you. Until it's you who needs a termination. Or until we who do fight, lose our battle. What then?

Today the war is outside these walls. Today we battle
to ensure every young woman in this state, in this
country, every single last woman who needs a
termination, gets it. That's today's ground. But if we
lose, tomorrow the ground changes. Today our cry is
freedom to choose. Tomorrow, it will be freedom to
teach, and to learn. To teach perhaps, that
terminations were once upon a time practised, not by
monsters, but by people, for people, that people once
believed in the quality, not just a quantity of life.
They won't stop there. If this 'moral' society prevails,
then again, the ground shifts. The day after
tomorrow, we will fight merely to think, privately.
To think, perhaps, that a termination was after all the
best solution we humans could muster to the curse of
our own hapless reproduction. A termination really
will have become unthinkeable.

Perhaps I'm being unnecessarily apocalyptic. As our
chair says, I have seen the enemy at fairly close
quarters, and yes, on that occasion I did choose to
duck a little late. Forgive my extravagance.

Argument. Debate. Reason. Commitment.
Lobbying. Statistics. Media. The ballot box. The law.
Self-defence. All these are tools of the modern
academic in pursuit of a good and I believe
genuinely moral society.

I did say this was going to be a brief speech – and
I did promise myself I'd make it badly structured –
If not now, when? So I'm going to finish with an
anecdote – about my father, who would on this day
have been very proud. In fact a friend of mine is
fond of telling me I've never quite escaped my
father's shadow. If light can have a shadow. Well, that
friend can't be here today. Here goes.

My father, Allan, was a general practice doctor in a
not very particular part of Edinburgh, Scotland. A
much maligned man, professionally, he formed the

opinion quite early that timid young girls were best raised on the plain facts. Facts unadorned. Un-excused. Sometimes, hardly even explained. A diet of these facts would, he believed, create a strong and determined mind. You can see why he was maligned. So, when one morning – I must have been nine or ten, perhaps eleven – when I woke to hear weeping and looked out to see a young woman, swaying slightly, in the road below, and saw the wet ribbons hanging there between her legs, he told me – the plain facts. Unadorned. Unexcused. The ribbons, he said, are her womb. The sticks in her hand – are needles. She has tried unsuccessfully, probably alone, to solve the greatest dilemma any woman will ever face. The dilemma of her own reproduction.

That woman's life, like my father's, was much too short. A truly moral society, would I believe have preserved it much longer.

Lunch, I think.

Delayed, uncertain applause. Lights fade.

Scene Eight

The basement, as before. FATHER D has set the tv up on the table, and is flicking from channel to channel with the remote. All the channels are snowy, with ghosted images of American football etc. JOHN is standing, watching FATHER D intently. There are food cartons around, and coke cans, one of which FATHER D is holding. He continues to flick for a while, then walks to the tv and adjusts the aerial.

FATHER D: I don't know what business they had upstairs. Meat wholesale or somethin'. They musta got steel walls in this place.
He stands back, but the picture is not improved.
Relax, John. They ain't gonna be back fer quite some time yet. You wanna nother coke, help yerself.

JOHN does not respond.

Know what sometimes goes through my head when I
see a ballgame like this? All them blobs in the crowd
there. Rest of the week, these guys are quietly goin'
'bout their business, keepin' their views to theirselves.
Weekend comes an' su'nnly they in the park, shoutin'
their opinions like a bunch a hucksters. What
happened to those people? Their views change all of
a sudden? Lord, if we could tap into that.

I reckon there's thousands might declare fer the cause
if they weren't so scared all the time.

I'm gonna try another channel here.

*The picture licks through channels and steadies on a
still very snowy picture of a ballgame.*

JOHN: Would you turn the tv off, Doctor Price?

FATHER D: Hold the faith brother John, this is not
gonna take another minute. Tell the truth, these
RICO laws, – 'bout the scariest thing yet. You know
they was brought in to deal with Al Capone types.
Great big organisations bent on extortion, murder,
who knows what else? Oklahoma friend of mine got
hit with a RICO action coupla months back. They
gonna take his house, his business, maybe lock him
up in jail too. Know his crime? He organised a demo
outside his local women's clinic. What they call
restraining trade. 'Cordin' to the state, that good
shepherd's the same as Al Capone, a man who
ordered the deaths of countless innocent people.
Sometimes I don't know how we got the face to call
ourselves God's country.

You wanna try some a them computer skills on this
thing or we gonna give up?

*JOHN has placed the chair centre stage, facing front, and
goes to his bag. FATHER D turns the tv off.*

FATHER D: Wass goin' on, John?

JOHN: Sit down, Doctor Price.

FATHER D: What?

JOHN shows FATHER D his ID. Pause. FATHER D stares at JOHN.

FATHER D: Well, John. I took a chance on you.

Beat. He switches the tv back on again. It continues to flicker, snowy with ghosted images.

JOHN: Would you sit down, please.

FATHER D: "I'm sure he's not one a them crazies, Angela. Quit worryin'." I guess I was lookin' under the wrong stone.

JOHN: I need ta know where Angela's headed.

FATHER D: I told yer all I know, agent. Plan was, Jacksonville.

JOHN: That's right. That's what you told me.

FATHER D: I guess that was a little deceitful. Strange. I decided you was okay in my mental head. Somethin' stuck.

JOHN: Where have they gone, Father D?

FATHER D: You got one a them things on you? What you call them, a wire?

JOHN turns off the tv.

Y'know, we're talkin' about a few, 'ornery people exercising their democratic right to protest, Agent Lemic. That why you come ta spy on a poor white trash girl an' a overweight black man?

JOHN: Where is Angela headed?

FATHER D: Doctor Price is my name. I'd be pleased if you'd use it.

JOHN: I have to warn you that as a federal agent I require your cooperation, Dr Price. I have that authority.

FATHER D: Russian Orthodox. Church an' state, hand in glove.

JOHN: Where did she go?

FATHER D: That who you afraid of here? Angela? You get it wrong, you get it wrong a long time.

JOHN: She told me 'bout the May Lake shooting. How you got her involved up there...

FATHER D: What exactly does 'involved' constitute here, agent?

JOHN: What do you think?

FATHER D: The FBI interested in what I think? Yer job is to prevent the expression of my thought.

JOHN: You encouraged her to take a job at May Lake.

FATHER D: (*Laughing*) Yeah well. Turns out you're both things Mr Lemic. FBI an' crazy. You honestly think I'd advise a girl like her – a young woman given an abortion in her teenage years – you seriously think I'd say 'Hey I gotta idea Angela – go work in an abortion clinic?'

JOHN: I think you might. If you wanted somethin' bad enough.

FATHER D: Such as?

JOHN: I don't pretend to know how you think. I think you might want information.

FATHER D: (*Laughing*) You know my favourite book, Agent Lemic? I published it myself 'bout a year back. Contains the names and private addresses of half the abortion doctors in the US. You wanna see the disk? See if it matches your list. See which medical practitioners better not try runnin' fer office? If Dr Bright up there is short of volunteers, we rejoice in that. We don't particularly wanna fill their vacancies for 'em. Know what I'm sayin'?

JOHN: You planted Angela in the May Lake clinic, and two people got shot. I'd say that's enough for a conviction.

FATHER D: Now let me tell you somethin' an' you listen up. When I found her, Angela was sittin' in a holdin' cell, shakin' like a leaf. She told me how she started workin' that place thinkin' it was a regular clinic, 'bout what happened to that boss a hers. Lord, she was such a mess in her emotions I thought she might not survive ta finish her tale. Now, if you persist with this, you are gonna destroy what the

Lord has rebuilt in her. That what you draw salary
for, John Lemic? Destroyin' the Lord's work in a
person's life?

JOHN: Would you describe Angela as a balanced
person, Doctor Price?

FATHER D: Hey, I know where thass comin' from.
Sure, Angela gets intense sometimes. There's a lot of
that around. I mean you can get intense about a
ballgame, thass okay. I happen ta believe intense is a
normal human reaction to the stuff we see here. The
evidence most persons are not allowed by their
government to see. And, if I may say, evidence
ignored by those charged to protect its innocents.

JOHN: You just provide that stuff right. Show that poor,
abused woman what a foetus looks like. Blood, and
gristle, and jelly...

FATHER D: Who said anythin' about abused, agent?
'Less you talkin' bout the routine violation of a
woman's body you call abortion...

JOHN: Doctor Price...
Give me the key, Doctor Price.

FATHER D: I'm sorry. I can't do that.
Beat.

JOHN: Angela says she worked at May Lake on your
say to get information and stayed on after to protect
OF and you in particular. Thass what she said. Thass
what she told me.

FATHER D: You can check this out. She was baptised
three months after joinin' OF. That was three and a
half, maybe four months after the shoot.

JOHN: You never knew her before that?

FATHER D: I am not going to repeat myself.

JOHN: So what is Angela even thinking of, saying those
things, Dr Price? Dr Price?

FATHER D: I only have your word she did.

JOHN: If you don't know what is going on in her head,
and she is headed for May Lake, you've got a

problem. Maybe it's true what people say about OF. Maybe iss just a cover fer what you really are.

FATHER D: I won't hear this. Till I talk to her, see whass going on, thass it from me.

JOHN: Yer an answer to prayer. Some crazy woman needs a new life – there you are. I hope you got a good headline fer that baptism. Yeah? Ex-Clinic Employee Says Yes To Life After Death?

Pause. JOHN puts on his jacket.

FATHER D: You goin' somewhere, agent?

Could be she has gone ta May Lake.

JOHN: What?

FATHER D: Marking the anniversary with a peaceful demonstration. Minibus takes half one way, the real crew goes ten minutes later. Kinda decoy system we have planned.

JOHN: Give me the key.

Give me the fucking key.

FATHER D: You're a smart young man, John. If you're right, you done your job, you worked it out.

JOHN: My job, reverend, is to stop wass goin' on here.

FATHER D: There's nothing goin' on here but democracy.

Beat.

JOHN: We're in a hurry.

FATHER D: Not me.

JOHN: We are both in this shit!

Beat. FATHER D makes no move. JOHN goes to his bedding/bag.

FATHER D: Somethin' went on here last night, didn't it? Ol' Angela, she was shakin' this mornin'.

I'm askin' you a question, agent. Did you mess with that girl?

JOHN: I don't have time fer questions.

FATHER D: And you think you gotta right ta judge her.

JOHN has retrieved his gun, and tucked it into his belt.

JOHN: Killers get the chair in this state. We both want to prevent that. Give me the key.

FATHER D: You know, you're right 'bout Angela, she's lowly. There's something broke off about her. One reason we got on I guess. Maybe it takes a person with not much future ta really want one fer others. The dumb ta speak, the deaf to hear...

JOHN: Will you fucking listen!

FATHER D: You know why they dumped the law on slavery in this land? Men finally decided they could not own and dispose of a life like it was a chair or a table. Like it was thing.

JOHN: I do not need... a lecture from you.

FATHER D: My wife chewed herself to sleep with thirty aspirin 'cause this nation sent our son ta die in a war she could not believe in. Now, I have never, ever believed violence would achieve the things I want to achieve in this world. But as a pastor, as a friend, even as the husband of a woman who OD'd herself ta death, unlike you, agent, I have the imagination to understand – that when a person feels betrayed by the law they trust in, they start to feel there is no way to do good, 'cept by forcin' themselves to do bad. Now I hope you're wrong about Angela.

I don't have anyone in the world I care so much about. But even if you're right about her and she is out ta harm that woman, your law is wrong. That means you're wrong, an' the fruit of your life will be wrong. I do have a key ta that door, and I'm sure you are prepared ta use violence to enforce the law you believe in. Well, you used pretty much everythin' else last night. I'm prepared fer the violence you will use, and I will resist. You know why? Because the law Angela is willing to kill for – assuming you're right, an' I don't believe you are right – that law, the Law of God, is better than the one you say you represent. The law whose already soiled reputation you dishonour.

JOHN: Is that it? You're under arrest, Doctor Price.

FATHER D: That right.

JOHN: And... I'd appreciate you giving me the key now.

JOHN has taken out his (empty) gun.

FATHER D: Y'know, I think Angela knows exactly what you are.

JOHN: Kneel on the floor, Doctor Price.

Kneel on the fucking floor!

JOHN has the gun aimed at FATHER D. FATHER D looks at him. Pause.

FATHER D: They ever tell you, John? Sometimes they almost deliver a child. The surgeon stands there, the head rests in one hand, the scissors ready in the other. Ready to puncture that skull, open it wide, and drain away that child's brain. And here you stand, defending the surgeon.

JOHN removes the safety catch. FATHER D slowly kneels on the floor. He begins to sing the hymn 'Oh Lord My God, when I in awesome wonder...' softly. A pause. JOHN throws the gun aside. He kicks FATHER D suddenly and violently. FATHER D keels over. JOHN begins to search his pockets for the key. Lights down.

Scene Nine

ROSEMARY's Office. Early afternoon. The pop of a champagne cork.

RICHARD: To a great speech.

ROSEMARY: ... which you missed...

RICHARD: ... a godawful lunch which I shoulda missed – and... Survival

ROSEMARY: Survival.

They drink. She takes off her jacket, revealing a flak-jacket beneath. Through the following exchanges she pulls the velcro straps and removes it. RICHARD fills his glass.

RICHARD: Hey, look what the well-dressed gynie's wearing this year.

ROSEMARY: Like it?

RICHARD: Is the pope a goalkeeper?

ROSEMARY picks up her glass/cup of champagne again.

ROSEMARY: Actually we're advised not to draw attention to anniversaries. Since Oklahoma. Cheers.

RICHARD: Pity – I got you a present.

ROSEMARY: Let me guess. Five startling new canvasses.

RICHARD: Spoken like a true agent.

Though wrapped, she knows its contents by its weight/shape. She might be about to open it, but he forbids her.

RICHARD: Hey. For the plane, doc.

ROSEMARY: Chocolates on a plane? Perfect.

We're toasting something else are we?

RICHARD: Whatever makes you say that?

ROSEMARY: I'm not sure. Something.

RICHARD: Well, no new canvasses. I got a studio by myself...

ROSEMARY: Congratulations.

RICHARD: Why thanks, doc.

ROSEMARY: I mean it. I'm pleased.

RICHARD: Yeah, me too.

Ron must be pissed you're makin' off like this.

ROSEMARY: It's called fact-finding. I need to see my mother.

(*Champagne*) Thanks for this. It's good.

RICHARD: Mother not managing, huh. (*Re: flak jacket*) You're not gonna leave your new skin behind, I hope.

ROSEMARY: Britain is a land very different from your own.

RICHARD: That famous British tolerance. As seen at soccer games.

ROSEMARY: We call them football matches. End of conversation.

RICHARD: Poor Professor Bright. All those free-debating academics clean wore her out.

ROSEMARY refuses to rise to the bait.

ROSEMARY: You seem more like yourself.

He pours himself more.

RICHARD: Here's to AZTs.

ROSEMARY: The indication is to drink heavily, is it?

RICHARD: The original medical breakthrough, doc –
booze and bombs, I recommend it to your angst-
ridden countrymen. Guaranteed to lighten the soul.
More?

ROSEMARY: No. Not for me.

Actually, I've changed my mind about British
tolerance.

RICHARD: You're fucked off with apathy too, huh...

ROSEMARY: It's not apathy. Something I've learned to
despise even more. We Brits refuse to join things up.

RICHARD: Ah-huh. You scan that stuff?

*She eyeballs him, refusing to confirm or deny, pushing on
with opening the letters and her opinion.*

ROSEMARY: On the other hand, neither do we waste
our time plotting the connection between a woman's
right to choose and say, taxation. Or the government
stance on gun law. Or the appearance of black
helicopters, or even – and to be frank, I almost regret
this – morality. At home terminations occur because
nobody's thought of anything better. And because
even thinking about the subject is painful, we hardly
talk about it. Let sleeping dogs lie.

RICHARD: Plus the Brits trust their politicians more,
right.

ROSEMARY: We trust them to be bastards individually,
as opposed to being part of some plan for world
domination. Of course I haven't been home for a
while. As I said, end of conversation.

RICHARD: Your approach to conversation remains
refreshingly autocratic.

He parts the blind of the window.

Wanna know the real difference? I heard this. It
always seems greener when you get off the plane.
Maybe it's the chocolates.

You er... you wanna buy a bike when you get back?
I could save it for yer. Lotsa big, wide, dry lookin'
open spaces for a gal to explore round here...

*Beat. Smile. She sorts the open envelopes from the letters.
Then glances at the screen and touches the keyboard.*

RICHARD: Well, think about it. I'd hate ta have ta give
it away.

ROSEMARY: No time to think. I've got an
appointment.

RICHARD: The Doctor is in today?

She goes to the filing cabinet.

ROSEMARY: Primary consultation. I said I'd squeeze
a few in before I left. Sorry.

RICHARD: Tell whoever it is, she needs a bike. Deal?

ROSEMARY: Tell her yourself. You'll pass her in
reception.

Support staff. Angela. Remember?

RICHARD: Domestic, right?

ROSEMARY: Very good. Better than me.

RICHARD: Support staff is what a domestic is called.
I speak the language like I was a native. Okay, I'm
outa here.

He makes to exit. She refers to the bottle.

ROSEMARY: Wait. Take that with you. And thanks.

RICHARD: I gonna see you before you go?

Beat.

ROSEMARY: When I get back, I think.

Beat.

RICHARD: The big goodbye, huh.

ROSEMARY: I don't do guilt, I told you. Thanks for
coming today. It was nice.

RICHARD: Me neither. Guilt, that is. Don't do. I...
I tell ya, I'm gonna work strictly in pastels from now
on. Who knows – might even dress in 'em, like Ron.

She goes to get the door. He catches her hand, holds it, kisses it. She makes herself reach out to him.

RICHARD: Watch out for those fucking foreigners, y'hear?

ROSEMARY: Thanks.

They part friends. He exits, opening the door for himself.

ROSEMARY: Leave the door open, would you.

RICHARD: (*Sotto, calling, a private joke.*) You know I was walkin' when I came in this place ...

She smiles – it's an old joke. The door swings shut. Pause. She picks up the pace again. She talks to the intercom.

ROSEMARY: Are these all the records we have, Suzy?

Suzy: (*Off*) Yeah.

ROSEMARY: Okay.

She sees the present again, and opens it. She takes out a chocolate, and eats it. She takes out a bunch of keys, and unlocks the desk drawer, to put the chocs in. She finds the gun. She puts it back in the drawer, with the chocs, and pushes it shut, but doesn't lock it. She walks to the window. She looks out, then faces back in, speaking to the room.

ROSEMARY: Honorary Professor. Not bad, eh?

She walks back to speak into the intercom.

ROSEMARY: Give me a couple of minutes Suzy...

A knock at the door. She speaks again to the intercom.

ROSEMARY: Never mind.

Come in.

The door opens a little.

Come in.

ANGELA appears in the doorway. She is pregnant, as before. In addition she wears a long black wig.

ROSEMARY: Angela.

I didn't recognise you.

Come in.

ANGELA enters. ROSEMARY shuts the door.

ROSEMARY: Can I get you a drink? Tea, coffee?

ANGELA: I don't take caffeine when I'm pregnant.

ROSEMARY: A cold drink?

ANGELA: I don't think so.

ROSEMARY: Fine – sit down. I'll be with you in a minute.

ANGELA stays on her feet. ROSEMARY taps the keyboard, looks at the screen.

ROSEMARY: Having a bit of trouble with this thing – here we go. Angela... finished here about a year ago. Bit less. Can't say I blame you.

ANGELA: Will you call me Perpetua? Thass my name now.

ROSEMARY: Alright. You're still Angela on here. Do you want me to change it? You'll have to spell it out I think.

ANGELA: P - E - R - P ... E - T - U - A. I think.

ROSEMARY: I've put it in brackets. Worked here one, nearly two years... came to us before with period pains. That's cleared up now. Were you prescribed the pill fer that?

ANGELA: I was, but I never took 'em. Lord answered my prayer all by hisself, I guess.

ROSEMARY: But this is the first time you've been pregnant?

ANGELA: First time since then. I was pregnant before once.

ROSEMARY: I have to ask you this. Did you choose to terminate that pregnancy?

ANGELA: I did terminate it.

ROSEMARY: When was that?

ANGELA: I don't know exac'ly.

ROSEMARY: Would you say it was two years ago, five years, more than five years..?

ANGELA: I'd say more.

ROSEMARY: It wasn't here?

ANGELA: It was some place somebody knew. Angela, that was.

ROSEMARY: I see. I'm sorry, we're usually more
thorough than this. We're up to date now.
I wouldn't normally have agreed to an appointment
without knowing you better, but since you feel
a connection here, that's fine. Besides it's nice to
see you.
I'm sorry, sit down.

ANGELA: I'll stand, Dr Bright. If that's alright.

ROSEMARY: If it's more comfortable.

ROSEMARY: How can I help?

ANGELA: I seen you on the tv a lot. They say you juss
got wounded.

ROSEMARY: Yes, the bullet passed straight through.
Someone up there likes me.

ANGELA: Don't look like you bin shot at all.

ROSEMARY: We're all trying to put it behind us.
Though I must say the bedrest did me the world of
good. Felt like a new woman when I came out. Now
there's just the struggle to look like one.
Pause.

ROSEMARY: How many months are you, Angela – do
you know?

ANGELA: Can you call me Perpetua?

ROSEMARY: Perpetua, yes, I'm sorry.
Where's that from, is it Spanish?

ANGELA: I think it's Roman.

ROSEMARY: Someone you've read about.

ANGELA: She was kind of a saint.

ROSEMARY: I see.

ANGELA: Issa person my daddy told me about. Plus
I like the sound a lot.

ROSEMARY: It's pretty.

ANGELA: Says she was beautiful in the book.

ROSEMARY: Yes.

ANGELA: I figure I got a pretty name, thass a start, right.

ROSEMARY: Right. You shouldn't worry about your
hair. Happens to a lot of girls. Grows back almost
always.

ANGELA: I call this my Perpetua look. She held it up
real high so they could see her swan-like neck.

ROSEMARY: I'm sorry?

ANGELA: Folks always wanna know the story. Usually.
Course, if I'm takin' up too much of your time, Dr
Bright...

ROSEMARY: No, that's fine. I'd like to hear it.

ANGELA: I wouldn't wanta impose myself...

ROSEMARY: Really.

ANGELA: She lived 'bout 300 AD. She had this long
dark hair like I said. They all wanted her ta bow the
knee 'cause she was a Christian only she wouldn't,
you know, worship Ceasar, n'all. Perpetua this is. So
they drag her behind a cart ta the place they done
gladiators an' stuff, told her again, but she told 'em
she wasn't gonna do it, her faith was so strong. Last
they tell this guy with a sword, one a them gladiators,
cut her head off. Perpetua, she don't flinch one tiny
bit. She lifts up her hair so's he can see her neck real
good, help him out. Poor guy juss can't do it, I mean
she's a beautiful woman. The crowd's gettin' uptight
by now; the emperor's gonna get this guy killed fer
not doin' his duty. So Perpetua, she lifts up her hand,
grabs his sword arm. Drags the blade cross her throat
till it splits like a cherry with the stone in it. Thass
how she died.

ROSEMARY: And that's the name your father gave you.

ANGELA: Suits me pretty good, I think.

Pause.

ROSEMARY: This pregnancy...

ANGELA: The baby, right.

ROSEMARY: Do your parents disapprove?

ANGELA: I don't see my folks much. Ma's dead
anyway.

ROSEMARY: But they're religious. Your father, you
said...

ANGELA: My father ain't what you might call a
Christian, Dr Bright.
Beat.

ROSEMARY: Who've you been seeing up till now.
What's your doctor's name?

ANGELA: I bin going the City, see whoever's there
mostly.

ROSEMARY: And they referred you here? I mean, they
told you how to get an appointment?

ANGELA: Folks talk 'bout abortion in this town they
mostly think of you. I forgot much as I could, once
I left, only you up there all the time. You said a baby
was like a li'l bomb tickin' away inside a person. You
remember that? Weird the way God speaks to a
person, huh?
Pause.

ROSEMARY: Angela... Let's go from the beginning...

ANGELA: Start again. Wipe the slate clean, right?

ROSEMARY: Ange... Perpetua... What is it you want
from me?
Why have you come here today? Let's start with that.
Beat.

ANGELA: I told you, Dr Bright. I heard this was the
place for terminations.
Pause.

ROSEMARY: Angela this pregnancy looks quite
advanced. Do you know exactly how many weeks
you are?

ANGELA: I don't think exac'ly matters a whole lot...

ROSEMARY: I'm afraid it matters very much. Have
you talked with anyone else about this? A counsellor,
a friend? The father perhaps?

ANGELA: I don't see my father 'less I have to. I said.

ROSEMARY: I mean, is there a boyfriend? One you
think might have made you pregnant.

ANGELA: I stopped doin' boyfriends, Dr Bright. Soon
as I found the Lord.

Beat.

There's John, I guess.

ROSEMARY: John.

ANGELA: He was juss one night, thass all. We all make mistakes.

ROSEMARY: And you think this John is the father?

Beat.

ANGELA: I don't think that could be possible.

Pause.

ROSEMARY: Perpetua, we have a counsellor attached to us here. Did you meet Sarah? I'm going to make an appointment for you to see her very soon. She's nice, you'll like her.

What about some time tomorrow?

ROSEMARY has picked up the phone.

ANGELA: I don't need a counsellor, Dr Bright.

ROSEMARY: Well, I think you might find it useful. Someone with a bit more experience at talking things through. Sarah will help you decide, clarify exactly... what it is you want to do.

ANGELA: I came to see you, Dr Bright. I thought you'd help.

Beat.

ROSEMARY: (*Phone*) No, it's okay.

ROSEMARY replaces the phone. Beat.

ROSEMARY: Angela I'm not saying I won't help you, what I am saying is this pregnancy is quite advanced.

ANGELA: I understand what your sayin'. You real short a time when some person don't want their baby killed.

Beat.

ROSEMARY: You've decided to continue this pregnancy.

Perpetua?

ANGELA: Had ta work real hard on the net, get it wired. Stop everyone from huggin' me. I look in the

glass on the way in, I know I done my job. Looks a
li'l advanced like you say. I don't have a baby, Dr
Bright.

ANGELA's hand is on the side of her belly.

ROSEMARY: Angela what is it you're trying to tell me...?

ANGELA: Where I got my finger, thass what you call
the detonating pin. We go up 'fore it starts ta ring's if
you press your panic 'larm button.

I think you should put your hands on the table now.

Beat. ROSEMARY places both her hands on the table.

ROSEMARY: Angela ...

ANGELA: Iss a bomb, Dr Bright. See, ah'm not afraid to
say it. I know where I'm going; I know why.

ROSEMARY: Angela. I think, if you'd wanted to hurt
me, you'd have done it by now. That's right, isn't it?

ANGELA: It's got real easy fer you, hasn't it.

Pause.

I don't need ta shoot straight, thass one thing this time.

ROSEMARY: What...?

ANGELA: If I did, they'd a juss changed the name on
the door, start over. I figure this way's better.

ROSEMARY: Good God...

ANGELA: Didn't think I had it in me, huh.

ROSEMARY: Get out. Out!

Pause.

ANGELA: I can't, Dr Bright. Ah'm layin' down my life
fer the unborn.

ROSEMARY: You passed him in the hall. In his
wheelchair. His legs won't work, there's no feeling.
Did you know you did that to him? Do you care that
he'll spend the rest of his life like that? Angela?

Pause.

ANGELA: I didn't mean that to happen.

ROSEMARY: Didn't mean...

ANGELA: We all make mistakes, right. I confess mine
ta the Lord and he is gracious and just and will
fergive us our sins.

Besides he chose to be here that day, doin' what he was
doin'. I don't think the unborn get a choice at all.

ROSEMARY: You almost kill a man, and you say you're
for... given...

ROSEMARY suppresses her anger.

ANGELA: It ain't too late for you neither, Dr Bright.
You can repent fer what you done here. I think
everyone should get the chance ta repent fer what
they done. Even you. You gonna do that? Only takes
a minute ta say a prayer.

Beat.

ROSEMARY: How many minutes?

ANGELA: There's no timer. Till I let go of this pin, we
okay.

You gonna repent?

Dr Bright?

ROSEMARY: I thought suicide was a sin.

ANGELA: It ain't suicide, Dr Bright. Iss what you call a
sacrifice.

ROSEMARY: And murder?

ANGELA: Justifiable homicide, Dr Bright. I'm killin'
you fer good reason, I think thass pretty clear...

ROSEMARY: I see.

People will miss you. Angela. Your parents...

ANGELA: You don't listen, Dr Bright...

ROSEMARY: Your boyfriend then. What about him?

ANGELA: I don't have boyfriends, Dr Bright. I said that.

ROSEMARY: I meant the baby's father. John, wasn't it?

ANGELA: There's no baby, there's no father, right.

I mean who's the doctor round here?

ROSEMARY: But John is your boyfriend. Won't he
miss you? You slept with him. You said so. One night.

ANGELA: I didn't intend fer that to happen.

ROSEMARY: I can understand that. An accident.

ANGELA: I don't think even John knew it was going
to happen.

ROSEMARY: You must be worried. I know I would be.

ANGELA: I'm prepared fer what I have ta do,
    Dr Bright.

ROSEMARY: I meant – worried in case you're
    pregnant. It's easy to forget about protection.
    Especially if you aren't planning it. And you aren't
    on the pill, are you?

ANGELA: I don't think...

    Pause.

ROSEMARY: Only if you are pregnant – or might be –
    there's not just our lives to consider. Is there?

ANGELA: I don't think that could be possible.

ROSEMARY: Have you had a test?

ANGELA: A what?

ROSEMARY: A test. To see if you're pregnant.

ANGELA: I don't consider thass necessary.

ROSEMARY: There's a very good chance of
    conception at your age. You're young, healthy – there
    could be a life started.

ANGELA: You're sayin' iss a life now? I thought it was
    just a blob a gristle you fetch out with a toothpick.

ROSEMARY: No, I... It's not what I say that matters, is
    it? It's what you say. If you're right. If you're right,
    it's a pre-born. A fully formed human. You won't just
    kill me. You'll murder an innocent.

    Beat.

ANGELA: Think yer clever, huh.

ROSEMARY: No, I'm just...

ANGELA: I know what iss like ta have a life inside, Dr
    Bright. I know how it feels when iss scraped out. You
    ever bin aborted you'd know that.

    Beat.

ROSEMARY: What makes you so sure I haven't? Been
    aborted? I'm the sort of woman who'd have any
    number of abortions, aren't I?

    Pause.

ANGELA: How many you had?

ROSEMARY: One.

ANGELA: You ever think about it? The baby?

ROSEMARY: Sometimes.

    Yes.

    Beat.

ANGELA: Make friends with the assailant, right?

ROSEMARY: No you're wrong...

ANGELA: I don't think you should look fer common ground 'tween us.

ROSEMARY: You don't think so.

ANGELA: There ain't no communion 'tween good and evil, Father D's clear on that point.

ROSEMARY: I see.

ANGELA: Are you gonna repent, Dr Bright?

    Pause.

ROSEMARY: Angela, can I...

ANGELA: See, I don't know how much longer I can hold out.

ROSEMARY: I was going to ask, if I could have some chocolate. May I?

ANGELA: What?

ROSEMARY: There's some chocolate in the drawer.

    A gift. Why don't we have some?

ANGELA: I don't eat chocolate when I'm preg...

    ANGELA stops herself. Pause.

ROSEMARY: So you do think you might have a baby?

ANGELA: You got me confused.

ROSEMARY: I didn't mean to...

ANGELA: Well I am...

ROSEMARY: Alright. It's alright.

    Pause.

ANGELA: My gran told me this thing one time? She said if a person has her baby scraped, or loses the chance fer one? She's like a house with no chair. There ain't no place ta sit down. You think thass right? About the house? The chair?

ROSEMARY: I don't know. Perhaps. I know we all need something gentle sometimes... Some comfort.

I'll get the chocolate, shall I? I can't imagine dying and not tasting chocolate again. Can you?

ROSEMARY starts to pull the drawer open.

ANGELA: God speaks through you so clear. I think you could be an angel.

ROSEMARY: What?

ANGELA: My baby's in heaven, Dr Bright. I don't have to imagine bein' without chocolate at all.

Will you pray now?

Beat. Blackout.

THE END